the Savvy Girl's
GUIDE TO MONEY

*This book is lovingly dedicated to
the memory of my mother, Adele.*

EMILY CHANTIRI

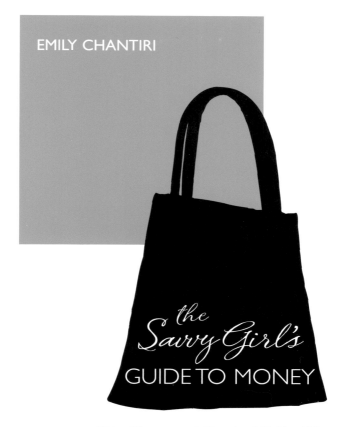

the *Savvy Girl's* GUIDE TO MONEY

Take Charge and Get the Life You Want

THUNDER BAY
P · R · E · S · S

San Diego, California

CONTENTS

$450

$595

$550

FOREWORD

I still remember the day I unfunded my future. I was about 25, and I'd recently started my first big job, as a news clerk at the *New York Times*. There was quite a bit of paperwork to fill out, including a form I was supposed to sign so that a little money from each paycheck would go toward my retirement.

Wait! Money withheld from each paycheck? Were they kidding me? I asked my supervisor if I had to sign this thing, and she said it wasn't required, but that it was a really good idea. *I don't think so*, was my only thought as I tossed the form—and thousands of dollars of future savings—in the trash.

That was the moment when someone should have handed me a copy of a book like *The Savvy Girl's Guide to Money*—if only it had existed back then. There comes a time in every young woman's life when she starts to realize that money matters but she doesn't want to read a lot of Wall Street-ese to get a grip on her finances.

That's when you need a book of commonsense money advice you can turn to, a book that won't fry your nerves with long charts or complex calculations, a book that delivers practical steps you can take right now to become the financially secure woman you know you can be.

That's right. You know you can do this. Heck, if I can find financial sanity after years of practicing the opposite, anyone can. And what Emily's book makes clear is that achieving your financial goals doesn't require mastering advanced mathematics but understanding your financial behavior so you begin to take control of your spending, saving, and basic investing.

I think what keeps women from feeling financially in control is the two-brain problem. One brain knows that you work hard for a living, that those paychecks aren't always as big as you would like, and that you want to live responsibly but happily. You want to pay the bills but still have a good time.

The other brain just wants to have a good time—and sneaks off with the credit card, forgetting about the car payment and saving for a home, and goes cruising in the mall.

Now the freewheeling brain has to face up to the irritated sensible brain, and the next thing you know, your stomach is in knots, you're picking a fight with your mom or your boyfriend, and you're not sure why.

Not that I've done that.

The good news is, as you'll see when you start reading, all the examples in this book deal with real-life women just like you and me. Women who love to shop but want to save for a vacation. Women who want their own homes but aren't sure how to get there. Emily talked to them about their problems and their goals—and how they figured out their own financial solutions. Did they hire stockbrokers and financial advisers and get a PhD in economics?

No, because you don't need all that to learn the basics of money management and make a whole lot of financial progress—and maybe even enjoy it along the way. For some people, money is scary and stressful, but holding onto the belief that money is *always* that way only creates unnecessary money problems. By learning a few simple, take-charge skills, you'll discover that money can even be kind of fun.

And you know what? You want to enjoy your financial life as much as possible, because it feeds so many parts of your life: your job, your home, your goals, your future. Like Emily, I work with a group of women called the Women in Red, dealing with everyday financial issues (you can find us online at the MSN Money Web site). I've seen people go from being financial stress cases to preaching the gospel of financial sanity.

So I can tell you, the more support you get for your own financial growth, the better you'll feel. The better you feel, the more you'll enjoy your money. The more you enjoy it, the smarter your financial decisions will be.

If I'd known that back when I was 25, I'd be a much wealthier woman today. Luckily, you've picked up this book at just the right moment in your life, so that you are now headed toward the life you want, and with plenty of money to get you there.

© MP Dunleavey, 2006

CHAPTER ONE

THE CINDERELLA CONSPIRACY

Once upon a time, there was a beautiful girl named Penelope. She lived in a penthouse with a view of the city skyline. In between manicures and lunch dates with her friends, Penelope loved nothing more than to shop.

And why not? Her handsome, loving, and rich husband, Robert, got just as much pleasure watching his wife max out her platinum card each month as she did spending the money. After all, the card was a gift from him for their first wedding anniversary.

The couple surrounded themselves with the latest clothes, fashion accessories, cars, boats, and trips to exclusive islands that the other half just dream about . . .

Stop right there.

This is where the fairy tale ends and the reality sinks in. If your life is anything like Penelope and Robert's, then this book is not for you. This book is for the rest of us, the millions of working women earning a living and trying to make ends meet.

We work hard, and we love life. We juggle our time with friends, family, jobs, and (if we're good that week) the gym. We love coffee dates with our friends, chatting about our latest romance—or lack of romance.

We're doing pretty well, and we need to, because there is no rich Prince Charming around the next corner.

Fairy tales like the one above do come true—just often enough to keep the women's magazines in cover stories. In 2004, Australia's girl next door, Mary Donaldson, married a real prince, and now she's Crown Princess Mary of Denmark. But that's one prince between about 10.3 million Aussie women. And, here in the United States, it's been more than fifty years since Hollywood actress Grace Kelly met and married her prince. Even if math isn't your strong point, you'll agree that these are fairly hopeless odds. Leaving princes out of it, you are very, very unlikely to find someone who wants to keep you without you lifting a finger. (And if you should happen to, how long will it be till he sets his sights on trophy wife number 2?) No, these days we want our own careers and our own money. It's the difference between being independent like Carrie in *Sex and the City* or being handcuffed to someone else's money, like Gabrielle in *Desperate Housewives*. Whether we're single or not, childless or not, we need our own incomes in order to have the lives we want.

Sure, it's possible for most couples to live permanently on one salary. You just can't live in a major city, you sure can't buy a home, you can't travel, you'll be shopping at Wal-Mart, and you'll be asking yourself if you really need to buy meat more than once every two weeks.

And even if you're footloose and fancy-free, there are plenty of everyday expenses. A working girl needs a working wardrobe, including hair, shoes, cosmetics, and accessories, all of which require frequent updating. Then there are after-work activities: more clothes, drinks and meals out, movies, gas, and weekends away with the gang. And we haven't even mentioned rent, groceries, or phone bills yet. It is very expensive being you!

But it doesn't need to be so pricey that you can barely keep your head above water. You'll be surprised how a few savvy tricks can change your lifestyle now, your future dreams, and the way you feel about yourself.

I know it's a bit eye-glazing to even have to think about money, let alone sit down to plow your way through a 401K statement. Don't worry, I understand that time is precious and attention is short. Trust me, if I ever forget, my sisters will remind me of that.

I wasn't born financially savvy. I had to learn, too. For me it started a few years ago with a book club.

Each month, I'd get together with a group of friends and have a wonderful meal, nice wine, and a chat about books, life, and love. We were a mixed bunch—some had families, some were single, some were highfliers, and others were just starting out. But we had one thing in common, which we spotted fairly quickly: none of us was money smart. Not even the ones who were in executive jobs, running big corporate budgets! In fact, I was the only one who had any investments at all, owning some shares.

But we all wished we felt more in control of things. So we revved each other up and decided to do something about it. We turned the book club into an investment club. We learned it all from scratch, and we did it together. It was great, and we were soon making money.

In fact, we did so well that I suggested we write our story. Four of us did, and the book—*The Money Club*—was a success. Three years later, we followed up with another winner, *Financially Fit for Life*.

So, there I am, with two books under my belt and a lot of strangers telling me how useful the advice had been and how it had changed their lives. But it was a different story in my own family. I'm one of five sisters (yes, the fights over the phone were endless when we were growing up). Two of my sisters didn't need any help; they were already on the way to money smarts. But my other two sisters definitely needed a hand. They had good jobs and were intelligent, but they found money boring to think about and embarrassing to talk about. So every month they found themselves down to their last cent.

Easy enough to fix, right? They just needed to take my advice directly from the books. I gave them each a copy. The reaction was the same: "Sure, I'll get around to it," meaning: as much as I love you, not in this lifetime.

Here's my sister Rhonda's take on what happened:

I can honestly say I was over the moon for Emily. I was telling everyone that my sister had written a book. But time really is an issue for me. I know everybody says that, but I start work at 8 a.m. and don't finish till late. At the end of the day, I just want to go to bed. I'll buy a magazine, and sometimes it will sit on the shelf for three weeks before I read it.

I just wish I'd read Em's books sooner.

In the past, I was used to being in relationships where I had no commitment. And when you don't have commitment, you are independent and you do things for yourself. I was with my previous boyfriend for four years, and we had separate bank accounts. It became obvious we were not going to stay together when he bought one investment apartment on his own, then another. He did not involve me in the whole process. Maybe I was too independent! Anyway, we separated and I was single again.

I started going out, started partying, and started spending. I was spending money on new shoes, clothes, bars, cafés, food, drinks, and the rest. I have always worked hard, but soon I was working weekends to make ends meet.

Now I'm in a committed relationship, and recently we got married. Three-and-a-half years into this relationship, we opened a savings account together. This was the first time I had to share my money. I was so used to having my money for myself.

We opened the account together because we were going to buy property.

I started to take my finances seriously, even buying a software package to do a "proper budget."

But those first two books of Emily's are still under my bed, gathering dust.

(Don't you just love her honesty!)

I always thought to myself, I should pull them out and read them and learn something, but still I didn't do it. But then she decided to write this book, for girls like me. I was her guinea pig, and now here I am after all these years of being clueless about money and having saved for my wedding and to my astonishment, my husband and I have just bought a home together. It's amazing how much difference it has made to understand about money at last, and to be able to use it to get where I want to be. **Rhonda, 34**

Rhonda helped me, too. By using her as my guinea pig, I figured out just what kind of help a girl who thought she could never get her head around money issues needed. Now she's so money savvy I just stand back and watch her go! If Rhonda did it, you can too.

CHAPTER TWO

SO WHERE DOES ALL MY MONEY GO?

The best way to understand where all your money goes is to break down a typical day in your life. We are going to start off with the little items first. Your daily expenses may look something like those of Sally, who is about to get a real wake-up call.

Sally is 31, single, and works for an architectural firm. After a big weekend—too many cocktails on Friday and Saturday nights and a movie on Sunday—Sally thinks to herself, "Thank goodness it's Monday, I can give my wallet a rest."

Let's have a look at a typical Monday for Sally.

8:00 a.m.	Weekly public transit pass	$20.00
8:30 a.m.	She grabs a coffee and bagel and heads into the office.	$6.00
9:00 a.m.	Her favorite magazine has hit the newsstands.	$4.00
11:00 a.m.	Someone in the office is going out for coffees;	
	they take orders for everyone.	$3.00
1:00 p.m.	Lunch (meal and a drink)	$8.00
6:00 p.m.	After that busy weekend, there's nothing in the	
	refrigerator for dinner. She buys Chinese takeout.	$12.00
	TOTAL	**$53.00**

Then Tuesday. Travel expenses and magazines are not on the agenda, so her daily expenses should be a lot cheaper, right? Unfortunately not.

8:30 a.m.	She grabs a coffee and bagel and heads into the office.	$6.00
11:00 a.m.	Someone in the office is going out for coffees.	$3.00
1:00 p.m.	Lunch	$8.00
7:00 p.m.	Last night, Sally stayed home. Tonight it's an early	
	movie and a quick bite to eat with a friend.	$25.00
	TOTAL	**$42.00**

Are things looking any better for Wednesday? Afraid not.

7:30 a.m.	Personal trainer	$30.00
8:30 a.m.	She grabs a coffee and pastry and heads into the office.	$6.00
11:00 a.m.	Someone in the office is going out for coffees.	$3.00
1:00 p.m.	Lunch	$8.00
	TOTAL	**$47.00**

As the week progresses, Sally's expenses continue. Thursday's expenses will look no different from the other days. Friday will be a killer on the wallet, as she starts the day again with her personal trainer and then in the evening goes out with her friends. It's fair to say her expenses for Friday will be double the other days.

Now let's see how Sally's costs are broken up for the week.

Before Sally has hit the weekend, she has already spent $288. This doesn't take into account buying cosmetics or clothes, or even spoiling herself with a facial.

Monday	$53.00
Tuesday	$42.00
Wednesday	$47.00
Thursday	$46.00
Friday	$100.00
TOTAL	**$288.00**

The scary thing is that Sally still has to pay rent, phone bills, and car bills. Oh, and by the way, we haven't started on her Saturday and Sunday expenses. No wonder Sally finds herself desperately wondering week after week where all her money has gone.

The good news is that just a few small changes can make a big difference. Let's start with a tiny change—cutting out one coffee a day. Hardly worth the sacrifice? Does knowing that this one simple change saves $780 a year make you feel differently?

This exercise really opened my eyes. It wasn't until I broke down all my costs that I could see where all my money went. I can't believe that I could save so much just by cutting back on one coffee a day; $3 a day is not that much, but it adds up when you are spending small amounts all over the place.

I really wasn't thinking, and I just got into the habit. I knew I was spending too much, but I just couldn't see where. I am going to start by cutting back on one coffee, and with the money I save I'll start to treat myself to a manicure once a week. **Sally, 31**

THEN THERE'S SAVVY GIRL SUSAN . . .

Meanwhile, across town is a savvy girl by the name of Susan. Susan is saving for a vacation at the end of the year. She figures she will need around $1,400 for a week in the Caribbean. This should be enough to cover her airfare, hotel, and meals.

Savvy Susan earns the same salary as Sally: around $35,000. She works as an office administrator for an accounting firm.

As you'll see from Susan's week, she is on target to save for her vacation.

MONDAY

8:00 a.m.	Weekly public transit pass	$20.00
8:30 a.m.	She grabs a coffee and heads into the office.	$3.00
9:00 a.m.	To keep up with news, she buys a paper.	$1.00
11:00 a.m.	Susan has recently discovered the benefits of herbal and chai teas. She buys them from the supermarket and takes a supply to the office.	
1:00 p.m.	Each time she brings her lunch from home, she knows she is a step closer to the Caribbean.	
6:00 p.m.	Having stocked up the refrigerator with plenty of groceries, she decides to make a lasagna, enough for two meals.	
	TOTAL	**$24.00**

It's the first day of the week, and Savvy Susan is already ahead of Sally by $29.

TUESDAY

6:45 a.m.	Half-hour run	
8:30 a.m.	Susan is late this morning and has no time for breakfast at home. No drama—she has a box of her favorite cereal at the office. She grabs a coffee and heads into work.	$3.00
11:00 a.m.	Herbal tea again	
1:00 p.m.	Lunch is last night's lasagna	
7:00 p.m.	Susan needs a night out. She and her friends take advantage of the cheaper evening movie deals, then grab a quick bite to eat.	$25.00
	TOTAL	**$28.00**

At the end of Tuesday, Savvy Susan is ahead by $43. What about Wednesday? Still on target.

WEDNESDAY		
6:45 a.m.	Power walk (and good catch-up time) with a friend	
8:30 a.m.	She grabs a coffee.	$3.00
11:00 a.m.	Someone in the office is going out for coffees.	
	Today, Susan needs a lift and has a second coffee.	$3.00
1:00 p.m.	Susan brings lunch from home, but she buys a freshly	
	squeezed juice.	$4.00
7:00 p.m.	Gourmet Club Night: It's Susan's turn to host, and she is	
	supplying the cheese and a bottle of wine. Everyone will	
	bring a dish to share.	$20.00
	TOTAL	**$30.00**

So far, she's ahead of Sally by $60.

As you can see, on average there's a difference of around $20 each day between the girls. On Thursday, Susan buys lunch and stays in the city after work for a drink with a friend who works nearby. On Fridays, like Sally, Susan wants to have fun and go out with her friends. Some of the best city bars offer happy hour between 5 p.m. and 7 p.m. The girls make the most of the cheap drinks, then usually go out dancing or clubbing. Susan will likely spend around $60. Including her coffee during the day and her share of a cab home, she'll have spent $72, a typical Friday for her.

Now, do you see where the money goes?

SALLY'S MONDAY TO FRIDAY		SAVVY SUSAN'S MONDAY TO FRIDAY	
Monday	$53.00	Monday	$24.00
Tuesday	$42.00	Tuesday	$28.00
Wednesday	$47.00	Wednesday	$30.00
Thursday	$46.00	Thursday	$24.00
Friday	$100.00	Friday	$72.00
TOTAL	**$288.00**	**TOTAL**	**$178.00**

Savvy Susan is "saving" $110 a week. That's $475 a month, or $5,720 a year!

I really don't feel as though I'm missing out on anything. I just cut back on some of the little things, and they all add up and really make a difference. I don't feel like I compromise at all. Compromising for me would mean no coffee or juice, or never going out. Or worse still, living on peanut butter sandwiches every week! **Susan, 31**

If Sally could cut back on a few things, in four months she could take a trip overseas or buy that DKNY dress she's been eyeing. Or treat herself to a manicure each week, or maybe a facial. The list is endless, and the savings are painless.

We've all had the experience of looking in our wallet and thinking, "Where has all my money gone? I withdrew $100 only yesterday."

This simple exercise will help you discover where your money is going. The time period over which you need to track your spending is one week—that's all. Just jot down what you spend day by day. Don't forget the $3 coffees and the other little bits and pieces. And don't think it's all just too hard.

Just think about all the time you've put in over the years counting calories and grams of fat, keeping food diaries, and doing complicated math to find out whether you could have that chocolate brownie or not. This is so much quicker and easier than that! Spend just a few hours one night this week doing it, and you'll find you will have already changed your life for the better!

HERE'S WHAT ANOTHER SAVVY GIRL HAS TO SAY

Brigitte is 24 years old and recently made a big move. She has set her sights on an overseas adventure.

I've recently moved cities, and I share an apartment with three other girls. The move has cost me quite a bit, but I have covered most of my expenses now.

I always take my lunch to work; that way I know what I'm eating. This can save me as much as $40 a week. I also walk home sometimes, and that way I get my exercise in. It takes me 50 minutes from door to door. I don't walk in the morning, because I don't like getting sweaty.

I think I'm fairly good through the week. I like to save my money and go out on the weekends. A night out with my friends costs around $60 to $80 for some food, drinks, and cabs. It's great when I can share cabs with friends, but that doesn't always happen. Even so, I don't have a car, so I figure I'm saving on that expense.

I buy really cheap shoes now. Once I spent $330 on a pair of boots, and three weeks later the buckle broke and I paid an extra $35 to get it repaired. I'm happy with cheaper shoes, and I'm really not into designer clothes at the moment. Don't get me wrong—I like them. I'm saving to go overseas; that is really more important to me than designer stuff.

Small things make a big impact

Brigitte's priority is an overseas trip, and she has learned how to cut back to make it happen. It's amazing how simple things, like cutting back on coffees, bringing lunch from home, and walking instead of taking public transportation, can make the difference between being able to go overseas or not, or buying a decent car or not.

Look at just two simple changes.

Cutting back on one coffee a day @ $3.00 = $15.00 a week.

Multiply $15.00 by 52 weeks: **Savings for the year: $780.00**

Cutting back on three bought lunches a week (the other two days you

can treat yourself) @ $8.00 = $24.00. Multiply by 52 weeks:

Savings for the year = $1,248.00

Total coffee savings $780.00 + lunch savings $1,248.00 = $2,028.00

If you are becoming ever more conscious of how the little things add up, you're in good company. Madonna is famously careful not to fritter away her fortune on unnecessary purchases, and Catherine Zeta-Jones—one of Hollywood's best-paid actors and married to a multimillionaire—says she's still "thrifty by nature."

If you are willing to cut back on three bought lunches a week and one coffee a day, you can save nearly $2,028 a year. What else can you painlessly cut back on?

SOME OTHER EVERYDAY ITEMS

	Daily	Weekly
Magazines		
Candy bars		
Gum		
Powerball and lottery tickets		
Cabs (when you are too tired to wait for the bus or train)		
Dry cleaning		
Bottled water and soda		
	TOTAL	TOTAL

LET'S GO TO THE EXTREME

Life wouldn't be worth living if we cut out all the things we enjoy. But let's take a look at what's possible.

We know Susan could save an additional $780 a year if she eliminated one coffee a day during the working week.

What about Sally? If she cut out both her coffees and brought her lunch from home, how much could she save in a year?

Cutting back on two coffees a day at $3 each will give her $1,560.00.

Cutting back on five lunches a week at an average of $8 each will give her $2,080.00.

Total saving: $3,640.00

Sure, this is an extreme case, and bringing your lunch every day may seem like you're back in grade school, but the point of the exercise is to show you how quickly little things add up. A couple of bucks here and a couple there—before you know it, you've spent the equivalent of a complete wardrobe update or an around-the-world plane ticket.

If you really do value a coffee every day more highly than seeing Paris or London, that's absolutely fine. But if you feel that no matter how hard you work you're barely staying ahead, then this is where to start. Cut out the little things you can do without, and the big picture will look a lot brighter.

It helps to have a goal. When I was 20, I wanted to travel overseas with a friend. We decided we would save for a year and then have four months exploring Europe. When I started saving, I was tempted many times to buy a new bag or go out for an extra night of clubbing. But when I felt myself wavering, I would say to myself, "I can get the real-deal leather handbag in Italy" or "I'll be going out to nightclubs in Paris." I kept picturing myself in those wonderful cities I had dreamed of, and the money went back in my purse.

My desire to see Europe and take four months off work was all the incentive I needed to get me there. And it was so worth it. Occasionally, my thoughts would wander back home as I sipped coffee on the Champs Elysées or while I was rummaging through the leather markets in Florence. I was so happy I'd stuck with my plan and saved. (By the way, did I mention the French and Italian men?)

What are the things you want to look back on with pleasure five or ten years from now? It all boils down to your priorities.

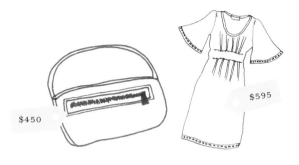

$450

$595

CHAPTER THREE

WHY DOES MONEY MATTER?

Well, first there's that whole hopes-and-dreams thing! Being able to have the experiences you want and own nice things is important for everyone. But being savvy about money is especially important for us women.

If being in debt doesn't worry you, your life must be a bit like Penelope's in our fairy-tale opening. Penelope is happy to max out her credit card because she knows her bills will be paid by her Prince Charming. The real world is different, and so are the lives of real women when the credit card bill arrives.

Take the following story from Linda. After a failed marriage, she realized that she alone had to take control of her finances, without a partner to help shoulder the debts.

Unfortunately, I was only married for a short time—three years, in fact. When my marriage ended, I realized it was really important to stay on top of my bills.

When there are the two of you, you can rely on each another if you are short of cash or if a bill needs to be paid. It didn't take long before I realized that I just couldn't go out and spend on everything I wanted. I'm the only one responsible for my bills now. I began to wonder if it was going to be like this all my life.

I'll admit, I did go on a spending splurge when the marriage ended. I just needed to spoil myself. Then the bills came in. That was sobering. I really felt out of control, almost fearful, insecure, and guilty.

Now, after being separated for over a year, I'm making it on my own again. I have a good job, and I feel like things are back under my control. I feel confident, independent, and secure. This is really important now, because I'm on my own. **Linda, 35**

These days, we have to be smart about our money, because we can't assume we're going to get married (let alone marry someone rich). In our lifetime, nearly a quarter of American women will never marry. And of the marriages that do occur, sadly, nearly half will end in divorce.

The reality will be that you may be on your own for a long time, and even if you do get married or have children, you will still need to work. With this in mind, it is clear why becoming financially savvy is important for all of us.

It doesn't matter whether you're in a relationship or are on your own—debt can affect us all. After a career move,

Natalie went on a spending spree that took her into dangerous territory.

I found myself owing a huge debt, largely due to moving to another state for my new job. I was really excited about the move, and I was looking forward to making a new start.

Unfortunately, I ended up buying a lot of new things and spending way over my budget. I was going out a lot, and because I work in the tourism industry, I took up plenty of travel offers. The offers were really good value. I guess I just went overboard. Also, before I moved to another state, I had to buy a car because my job involved lots of driving. I applied for a $6,000 loan and bought a secondhand car.

After finding a new place to live, setting up the condo with new furniture, and adding this to my monthly car and credit card payments, I found my bills were getting out of control.

The debt I had gotten myself into started causing me lots of stress, and I couldn't believe how quickly it had mounted up. The worry I had over how I was ever going to pay the debt caused me to get really depressed, and I couldn't sleep at night.

Luckily, a good friend suggested I go to my bank and see if they would extend the loan that I already had for the car. I was so grateful to the bank when they extended my loan and I was able to pay off the big bills, like my credit card and rent, which at the time were overdue by a few weeks.

I felt as if the whole world had lifted from my shoulders. Now I don't lose sleep at night; I realize I just went overboard. I don't want to be in that situation again. **Natalie, 33**

It's great to see that Natalie has bounced back and is getting her eight hours of beauty sleep again. Like Linda, her sense of security returned once her finances were under control. Natalie's story is also a good reminder that if you do find yourself in a similar situation, you too can turn things around.

There is no magic number—no dollar figure—that implies you are in debt. That's because, as Natalie found, debt is when you are living beyond your means. It's not the amount you spend or what you spend it on; it's whether you can afford to pay it off. For example, you may have a debt of $2,000 or more on your credit card, but if your salary comfortably allows you to pay this off at the end of the month, you're okay. If not, you are probably living beyond your means.

A much, much bigger debt—say $250,000—can be okay if that debt is a mortgage and you are making your payments each month. Why? Because you are investing in your future.

It all comes down to you taking a good look at your own financial situation. To understand how you got there, you need to look at the way you think about money.

MONEY BELIEFS

Have you ever thought about where your money beliefs come from? Were your parents conservative or careless with money? Perhaps they never spoke about it. Perhaps they made you budget your allowance as a child.

Either way, rightly or wrongly, their beliefs may have influenced the way you handle your money.

For example, even though Julie doesn't regard herself as a money whiz, she has a father who made certain she developed the essential skills for practicing good money management.

I wouldn't necessarily say that I am good with money, I just don't like being in debt. I've never had a student loan, bank loan, or car loan, because I have never bought anything that I couldn't afford. I could happily live without a credit card. My dad always warned me about credit card interest rates and being in debt. He didn't believe in handouts, so I was never given any and I had to work for my allowance when I was little.

It must be the way I was brought up, as I have learned to clear my credit card debt each month and I always pay my bills on time, so in that regard I never worry about money too much.

My partner is exactly the same, which makes our relationship easy. Neither of us is a big spender. We each pay our own bills, and we pay the mortgage together. **Julie, 31**

Michelle has quite different habits. Now 26 and working for a fashion magazine, she has spending patterns that were entrenched from a young age.

Growing up, I always loved clothes. I would save all my allowance, and I would buy the latest clothes, lipsticks, anything that caught my eye. I had to have it. Today, things are not so different. I work for a fashion magazine, and I am always surrounded by beautiful clothes, shoes, and the models who make them look so great.

I have a wardrobe full of designer clothes. I love Manolo Blahnik shoes and anything by Vera Wang—not that I can afford her clothes. But I would happily spend $800 on a pair of shoes I like. I'll walk into a department store and spend silly amounts like $200 on a handbag or some lingerie. I say to myself, "Just look." But it is so tempting.

A couple of years ago I got into debt, so I took out a loan to pay off my credit cards. I had three credit cards, and each one was carrying around $5,000 debt, almost $15,000 in total. I went to the bank and got a personal loan. The interest rate on the loan was much lower than my credit card rate. It made sense to take out the loan and pay off my credit cards. I was surprised how good I felt, because I knew that I would pay off the debt within a year. There was no way I could have gotten on top of my credit card debts in a year if I hadn't taken out the loan.

Once I paid off the debt, I kept two cards and canceled one of them. I figured that two cards would help me stay in control. When I had three I felt I had lots of money to play around with. It was just too tempting.

Now the two cards I have are getting up again. At least I know I could always go and get another loan. **Michelle, 26**

Michelle's and Julie's stories show how much money affects your life and your chance to be happy. But they show something else, too—how your past habits can predict your future ones, unless you are careful.

If you are feeling out of your depth and finding your spending habits are getting you down, you are not alone.

Sandra has realized her financial status has a big effect on her happiness.

I can tell you that the number-one feeling for me when I am in debt is depression and feeling limited, always having to budget.

It's awful not having the freedom to get something that you see advertised or you need. You watch other people in shopping malls or on the streets with nice houses, clothes, and cars, and it's depressing.

You start to tell yourself that you could do better. But the reality is, it's been the same for years and your hope diminishes because it seems so ongoing.

But when I pay my bills and pay my loan, I feel like I have made progress, even if it's only for a short time.

It is such a great feeling to pay bills and be on top again. Just having money to buy something or even to go to the movies is a huge pressure release. **Sandra, 29**

While it's great that fashion-addict Michelle took the initiative and paid off her credit card debt by taking out a personal loan, her pattern of overspending is emerging again. And Sandra is making an effort, too, but her old habits are still dogging her, making her lose heart.

You can't fool yourself by saying, "It doesn't matter if I'm hopeless with money now. It'll all change. I'll wise up in my 30s, 40s, or 50s." It's a slippery slope to anxiety and unhappiness.

So how do you avoid that?

You might feel one day you are on top of the bills, then the next day you're not. It's the money equivalent of yo-yo dieting: two steps forward, one step back. How many times have you tried to go on a diet and failed? I know—too often to count. But if you felt you absolutely had to lose weight to fit into a wedding dress, or a bikini for a special beach vacation, you would. It's all about your priorities and goals. Money works the same way.

Ask yourself, "Do I want to keep having the same issues throughout my life?" And more importantly, "Can I ever change?" The answer is yes, of course you can.

HOW TO BREAK YOUR BAD MONEY HABITS

Remove the temptation to shop

I understand it's hard if you work in a big city or in a place surrounded by boutiques and department stores and you're wandering around every lunchtime being tempted. So what could you do instead?

- Read a book or a magazine in the park.
- Grab a coffee with a friend (this is still cheaper than shopping).
- Go for a walk—get your daily exercise in.
- Pay bills rather than create them. Bank online or by phone and get it out of the way.

The no-touch bank account

Set up a secondary bank account and have money automatically taken out of your pay and put into this account every payday. If you don't have the money in your hands, you're less likely to spend it.

Write down your goals, keep them nearby, and check them regularly

The idea is to keep you focused on what you are saving for, whether it's a vacation, a party, a car, or a condo. Cut out a photo of what you're saving for and put it on a wall, near your desk, or in your wallet. My next goal is a trip to Hawaii, so I have a photo of a tropical island as my screen saver.

Take only a small amount of money with you each day

Once you get into the habit of taking only a small amount of money with you, you'll find you spend less without even noticing.

Leave your credit cards at home

Again, remove the temptation. The world won't stop!

Power to the friends

If you and your friends are in the same boat, then start working together and supporting each other. Check on one another's progress. You can do this even if you're all just trying to avoid accumulating more debt. But it's even better if you have a shared goal to work toward, like a luxury weekend away or even an overseas trip.

If your goals are the same, you can track your savings together and encourage one another through the tough spots. When I went traveling with a friend, we did just that, continually tracking each other's progress. We had a set amount that we had agreed we both had to reach before we could start our adventure.

Family support

Do you have a close family member or friend who is good with money? If you do, then make a time to talk with them. Ask for some practical tips. If they know you well enough, they may offer some tailor-made advice. Even just having them listen to your plans and act as a sounding board can be very useful. I do this with my family and friends, and I find it's really helpful to talk.

Just by making new spending habits today, you will change your future. Leave your old bad habits behind.

GOALS AND NECESSITY

My sister Rhonda was a classic spender. She loved clothes, nightlife, traveling, and going out to movies and concerts. You name it, Rhonda spent her money on it. It wasn't until she decided to commit to her relationship that her priorities suddenly changed. These priorities helped Rhonda form new habits that would take her into the future. At the age of 31, her goals suddenly changed. She wanted to buy a new car and a two-bedroom condo, and pay for a wedding. Within three years, she has accomplished all three.

In 2002, my boyfriend asked me to marry him. Well, that scared the heck out of me. After six years together, I just thought, "Why get married? We don't have any money, we have hefty credit card debts between us, and we're still renting. How on earth are we going to afford a wedding?"

I got some coaching from Emily, and with her came up with a plan. "Right," I said, "First things first. We have to get our financial act together to be able to afford a wedding." We bought some simple money-tracking software and made a budget to see how much we needed to put away. Whoa! Even scarier than the thought of getting married was how much we needed to save! The wedding would have to wait for another 18 months.

We put the brakes on our spending and started doing things like shopping on the weekend so we had food for dinners and lunches. We bought snacks to take to work from home, and eating out was cut down to once a week.

We used to like having breakfast out most mornings. Instead, now we just have a coffee out together. The savings were really significant. Just the two of us cutting back on lunches saved $100 a week!

After getting used to the changes, including not having much money in our pockets, we started to see a dramatic increase in our savings. We were putting $100 away each week into an online savings account, and we did not touch it. The interest it earned helped, too. We were still enjoying ourselves socially, but within a few months we could see a big difference. We were saving so well, I guess we got more confident about our ability to keep going, and we decided to look at property. So at the beginning of 2003, we approached several lenders and they all told us that we did not have enough saved for a deposit. But because we were paying off our debts quickly, our credit scores were improving and if we continued we could aim for an even lower interest rate. This was a huge motivation, and by mid-year we had $30,000 saved.

For someone who took 34 years to get her act together, I didn't do too badly! Now that I have all this, I think to myself, "I can afford to spend some money." But then I say, "What for?" This discipline is now instilled in me to keep that money growing for bigger things. **Rhonda, 34**

Rhonda's story is a classic example of how a person can change her past spending habits. Fantastic! Now I just have one more sister to convert . . .

Remember, no one is born savvy. I certainly wasn't. People change, and the two most common reasons for changing are chosen goals and necessity. Rhonda's reason was her goals. She could picture a new life that she wanted badly enough to change all her old habits and make happen.

For others, it is a matter of necessity. The necessity in my case came from suddenly losing my job.

When I was 30, I was working for a leading advertising agency and my career was progressing wonderfully. I enjoyed my job and the challenges it presented. Rumors were rife within the agency that 11 people were about to lose their jobs, but the account on which I worked was thriving, so I believed my job was safe. I can laugh now, but how naive I was then. You won't be surprised to learn I was one of the 11, but I was completely shocked—it didn't make sense. I found myself without a job but with a mortgage, and to make things even more interesting, I discovered I was pregnant with my first child!

In the end, I'm not sure whether it was through luck or perseverance, but I managed to find freelance work throughout the pregnancy, even if the work was sporadic. If it wasn't for the lessons I learned, being laid off would be a time in my life I'd rather forget. I felt weighted down with an overwhelming sense of financial uncertainty. What if my partner had lost his job? How would we have managed? The outcome was that I became determined to get my finances under control, and that's when my interest in investing began. I never wanted to be in that situation again. So for me the trigger to becoming financially savvy was necessity.

Sometimes life throws something unexpected your way, and you may find you need to cut back due to a change in your lifestyle, like losing a job, getting ill, or becoming pregnant before you had planned. With some good advice and determination, you'll be able to see yourself through these hard times.

Still, if I had to choose between goals and necessity to motivate me to become savvy, I would definitely choose goals!

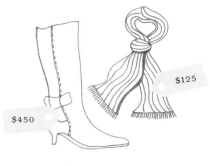

$450

$125

CHAPTER FOUR

CHARGING LIKE A WOUNDED BULL

Be honest, does your credit card bill make you feel a bit sick? Once you've taken a quick look at the amount due, do you stuff the bill away somewhere and try to forget about it? It doesn't take that long for bills to creep up, as Natalie found when she relocated to another state.

Big expenses like moving can do it, but so can updating your wardrobe too often, splurging at Christmas, or even just letting everyday bills mount up. Before you know it, you're over your limit and going backward. And, to make matters worse, you've put your credit score in jeopardy.

A SCORE WORTH KEEPING

Making regular payments to your credit cards, and ideally paying them off, will ensure you keep your FICO score high. Other payments such as car loans and insurance will also contribute to your credit score. Typically, the interest rate advertised is always based on a good credit score. That's why you'll always see the lowest rate quoted first, usually around 9.9 percent OAC (on approved credit). Lenders such as banks and credit card companies use credit scores to manage the risk posed by lending money to consumers. Without a good score, you'll incur higher interest rates. For this reason alone, it's important to keep on top of your credit card bills and other payments, ensuring you get the lowest rate available. The median FICO score in the United States is 723—how does yours compare? Check your FICO score at www.myfico.com.

The term "credit card" has bothered me for some time. I think it's a total misnomer. How can it really be credit when the card is used to carry debt? Perhaps if we called it a "debt card" people would understand what they are dealing with: a credit card is really just a collector of debts that need to be paid off monthly.

Maybe a "financial health" alert similar to those about smoking and drinking should be imprinted on your card:

Warning: overuse of credit cards may cause bankruptcy.

The problem with credit cards is that you don't see the exchange of cash. Imagine you have $500 in your wallet. With each purchase, you see the money dwindling. Once there is no more cash, it's simple: there's no more spending. With a credit card, the money is invisible. You hand over your credit card, you take your purchases, and the friendly salesperson returns your credit card intact. Nothing lost, but plenty gained as you happily walk out of the store with your bags of goodies—until the dreaded bill arrives weeks later, and suddenly your spending becomes a reality.

I don't know how many times I looked over my monthly credit card bill and only then remembered a particular purchase: oh yes, that book/dress/tank of gas—that's right, I put that on the card. Suddenly, reality would sink in as my eyes scrolled down the list; once again, I'd spent more than I imagined. You've probably had similar experiences. Maria certainly has.

Maria loves clothes, and she's paying a big price for indulging this love. High interest is keeping her from reducing her credit card debt.

I've got $4,000 debt on my credit card, and I never manage to clear it. I think I pay around 17.9 percent interest on the card, and I'll try to put a little bit on each month.

I love clothes—I'm a bit of a fashion victim. I buy my clothes from boutiques, eBay, and from the markets. I recently bought a pair of shoes for $15 from eBay. It was a risk, since I didn't know whether they would fit, but for $15 I took the risk and it paid off. I'll buy two or three pairs of new shoes a year also, and I'll spend around $250 or $300 for each pair.

I do mix expensive things with cheap things; you can do that with today's fashion. I don't earn much, but I do like clothes and that's where most of my money goes.

I share a one-bedroom apartment with my boyfriend, and we pay around $1,100 a month. We have been together for seven years, and he is a better saver than I am. I just can't seem to save at the moment, though in the past I have saved for a trip to Mexico. So I know I can do it if I really want to.

My boyfriend would like us to save for a deposit on a condo, but I don't know if I want to give up the things I enjoy. It was different when I was saving for the vacation, as it was only for a short time. If we buy a place, I feel like I'll be cutting back for 20 years or so. **Maria, 25**

SAVVY SOLUTIONS

Maria is carrying around $4,000 on her credit card from one month to the next, and she's paying around 17.9 percent interest to do it. If she just maintains this debt without adding any new purchases, she will be paying $716 a year in interest alone, without making any headway in paying off that existing debt.

There are a lot of things Maria could do with that $716 that would be far better than adding it to bank profits. It would cover the cost of several pairs of shoes each year, without compromising, or one month's rent, or a weekend away with her boyfriend.

It's great to see that Maria is not afraid to buy cheaper clothes if she really likes the look. But she does need to rethink her other financial choices. If Maria can't pay off her credit card, then she will find it hard or impossible to ever buy a condo. It's very important to pay off your debts before you even consider investing.

So what can Maria do right now?

By changing to a credit card with a lower interest rate, she can instantly save hundreds of dollars a year.

By rolling her $4,000 debt over to a credit card that charges 4.95 percent for six months and then 12.4 percent for the following six months, Maria will pay around $347 in interest payments instead of the $716 she was paying on her old card. That's already a savings of $370, just by swapping cards. As Maria has continually kept up payments on her credit card, she is able to swap to a card with a lower interest rate due to her good credit rating.

HOW MUCH INTEREST DO YOU PAY ANNUALLY?

It can be quite a shock to discover you are paying hundreds of dollars each year in interest. Amanda did the math and got a nasty surprise.

Due to a change in my finances and pay, I was using my credit cards for just about everything, even for purchases as low as $10 or $12. I had two cards, and over the course of six months my bills escalated and I had reached my cards' limits. I was finding it hard to pay my interest, which was more than $100 a month, let alone the whole bill. I then realized that over a year I had paid roughly $1,000 in interest. I was horrified because when I thought about it, I could have paid for a short vacation.

I decided to change to a credit card with a lower interest rate. So I swapped my credit cards, which had an interest rate of 16 percent, to a lower credit card deal. It had an introductory offer of 4.95 percent for the first six months, then 12.4 percent after that. I consolidated the two debts I had on my old credit cards to the new one.

Swapping to the lower rate gave me the time I needed to get back on track without the added stress of that high interest rate each month. Credit cards are great, provided you trust yourself to make your payments a priority. **Amanda, 37**

If you don't know how much you are paying in interest, then get your most recent credit card statement and check it as soon as possible—the interest rate should be stated there. (If you are still not clear, call your credit card company and have them clarify it for you.) It should also tell you on the statement how much you owe in interest for that month. Multiply that figure by the number of months you've carried that debt over, and you'll see the price you are paying for the card.

A number of credit card institutions are now offering no interest at all for the first 12 months, then around 12 percent after that and no annual fees. These institutions want your business so much they will offer you a "honeymoon" rate so you can transfer your existing debt onto your new credit card and pay really low rates on that amount for a set period, often one year, then pay a rate that is higher than this but still lower than your old card.

So if you are being charged anything above 16 percent interest and you're not clearing your whole debt every month, do something about it right away. It's crazy to be making money for the banks when you don't have to.

As an example, if you have been paying 16 percent interest on a debt of $2,500, you can save around $250 just by transferring that balance to a new card with a "honeymoon" rate or a year free of interest. If you have more than one credit card, you can consolidate them all and transfer the amount, saving you hundreds of dollars.

Currently, AT&T offers a zero percent interest rate for the first 12 months, then it jumps to 11.75 percent. This is still a good deal. Others offering similar deals include Citibank, Discover Platinum Card, and Bank of America Secured Visa.

Compare credit card rate offers at www.bankrate.com.

SOME OTHER THINGS YOU CAN DO RIGHT NOW

Use the power of negotiation

With many customers now transferring their credit card debts to get better deals, the major institutions are now willing to negotiate to keep customers. So even if you end up not switching, you can probably get a better deal, like Jenna.

When I called American Express to cancel my card, the lady I spoke to wanted to know why. I explained to her that I wanted to get a card with a lower interest rate and told her a friend had just applied for a credit card with a lower interest rate and recommended it to me.

I couldn't believe it when she then said that I had been a good customer and they were willing to forgo my late fee and my yearly membership fee if I stayed with them. Then she offered me two movie tickets on top of that. I figured that this saved me a late fee of $40, and the annual fee of $65, plus throwing in two movies tickets worth $20. The total came to $125.

I decided to stay with Amex because I thought she was doing her best to keep me as a customer and $125 was not a bad saving in fees for a year. **Jenna, 32**

This is not an isolated incident, so strike while the iron is hot. Let your card provider know you are shopping around, and you might be pleasantly surprised by what they offer.

Credit Infocenter at www.creditinfocenter.com has many examples, including consumers who were able to have their annual credit card fee waived, or get other fees or costs lowered. Check it out and pick up some negotiating tips.

A PLASTIC CARD WITHOUT THE INTEREST?

There is an alternative to credit cards—a card that doesn't come with interest. It's called a debit card.

Debit cards are issued through major credit card companies such as Visa and MasterCard. They offer similar benefits to credit cards in that you don't have to carry wads of cash around. You can still pay your bills by phone or Internet, and use them just about anywhere in the world, including to withdraw cash from ATMs in other countries.

The only difference is you will need to have the card linked to your bank account with sufficient funds to cover your spending. That way you never have debt. The card accesses the money directly from your account. As with a regular credit card, you will receive a statement at the end of the month, listing all your purchases. It's like your ATM card, except you can use it in a lot of situations, such as buying online, where you can't use an ATM card.

Danielle found that a debit card works for her:

I don't have a credit card, what I do have is a multiaccess card with debit card access. So many times I have heard my friends complain about having $3,000 to $5,000 in debt on their credit cards and how they can never pay it off. What makes it worse is that their cards have been fluctuating like that for years.

For me, I believe if I don't have the money then I shouldn't be buying. I also believe in out of sight, out of mind: if I don't have a card, then I don't use one. I just don't get tempted. **Danielle, 25**

Perhaps my father has the right idea . . .

At the age of 77, my father was given an application by a store he regularly visits for a store credit card. He was so baffled by the idea that it took us a long time to even explain the concept. He just couldn't understand that the card was used instead of money.

> *"Don't I pay for the clothes when I buy them?"*
>
> *"No, Dad, you hand over the credit card, and they will put it on a bill and send it to you at the end of the month—then you can pay for it."*
>
> *"That's all I do, I don't hand over any money to the salesperson?"*
>
> *"No, Dad, that's why you have the card."*
>
> *"But I have to pay for it in a month? What's the use—I may as well pay when I'm there!"*

Hard to argue with, when he put it like that . . .

MANAGING YOUR CREDIT CARD

Credit cards are inherently useful. They allow us the freedom to make purchases when we are caught short. And should your wallet get stolen, it's relatively easy to cancel your credit cards but just about impossible to recover a wallet full of cash. Also, for convenience when traveling overseas, credit (or debit) cards are essential. It's almost impossible to buy via the Internet without a card. And, with more people working on short-term contracts, credit cards are very, very handy for bridging the gap between job payments. That's okay, as long as you are committed to paying off the cards once your next job comes through.

"Sure, my card debt is high, but I'm still saving."
You are probably thinking that you are doing the right thing by having some savings. That's certainly the case if you have no debt. But it is really important to pay off any credit card debt first—otherwise you pay more in interest than you make on those savings.

I do understand why it seems like a good plan to save: putting money away regularly on the one hand feels like it counters the debt you have on the other. You feel you're doing something right instead of just slugging away paying off debts only to end up back at zero. But in fact it doesn't make sense to have savings in the bank earning interest at 5 percent while you are carrying around a $2,500 credit card debt at 16 percent interest. Let's say you have $2,000 in an interest-bearing savings account that pays 5 percent annually. This will pay $100 interest and will give you a total of $2,100 after 12 months. But if your credit card is carrying $2,500 every month and you are paying 16 percent interest, the interest charged for the year will be $400.

The $400 interest you pay on your credit card is, in fact, eating into your savings. Your $2,100 is actually worth $1,700 because it's cost you $400 to make that extra $100. All your hard-earned interest (and more) has been lost because you have not paid off your credit card.

If you're in this situation, put this book down right now and transfer any savings toward paying off your credit card.

Check your fees as well as your interest rates

If you're even a day late with your credit card payment, you could be liable for a penalty payment of $25 to $35. The same applies if you don't pay at all that month or, worse still, if you're even a few cents under your minimum required payment. So check what you're responsible for, and at worst, make at least the minimum payment to cover you until you can sort things out.

Are you paying extra for frequent-flier points?

Then there are annual fees and "loyalty program" charges. Some credit cards offer no annual fee, and some come with added bells and whistles such as frequent-flier points, for which you'll pay extra. If you are racking up big bills (and paying them off) and you can see the benefits of the points you earn, then you may feel the fee you are being charged is justified. But in an era of cheap domestic flights, it may not be worth your while if the points you earn barely cover a domestic flight, particularly if you are charged $45 or more annually just to be part of the reward program.

Let's take a look at this example with Continental Airlines. Once you sign up to be part of their frequent-flier program, you'll get your first free domestic U.S. ticket at 20,000 miles. Then you can expect to earn 15,000 miles after your first purchase. From then on, every dollar you spend will equal 1 mileage point, so it's going to cost you $5,000 to get a ticket worth $300. This is on top of the annual fee of $85 and an interest rate that starts at 7.99 percent for the first six months and then jumps to 17.99 percent on a variable rate. It seems a lot of money to spend before you can redeem your mileage points, when you consider it will cost around $200 for a flight from New York to Miami. You'll find plenty of cheaper options by searching online for the best available airfare. Also, it's worth noting that airfares are generally cheaper if you can plan in advance.

A card without an annual fee and a fixed rate is a much better deal.

Bear in mind that you'll find much cheaper airfares as airlines compete for your dollars and continually offer discounted fares. Do some basic math and decide for yourself whether being part of a frequent-flier reward program is really a privilege or not.

Other points programs

With the frequent-flier novelty wearing thin, many people are seeking loyalty points programs that can be used for other types of purchases. Some of these are very worthwhile, and the range of products available just keeps increasing. If you own a car, then you may find some credit cards, like the Citibank Platinum Select card, offer rewards points on auto insurance. You can also redeem points for household appliances with some cards, or get deals on wine and other items. Deb explains how she makes the most of her points:

I have a credit card with a loyalty points program. It's three points for every dollar spent, and the points can be redeemed for quite a large range of things (at gas stations and restaurants, for office supplies, auto insurance, rebates on travel, or gift certificates).

The card costs me $48 a year in annual charges, and the redemptions start at 1,600 points. Most of the things I want are around 7,500 to 8,000 points. That covers a $50 auto insurance rebate or a $50 gift certificate, for instance. I definitely wouldn't use the card just to accumulate points—having to spend $7,000 to get $50 back isn't smart, if that's all you're getting out of it. But with the way I use the card, the points are a bonus.

I pay for gas and restaurants and so on with it, and use it to pay big bills like insurance and the occasional vacation. And I pretty much pay it off each month. The interest rate is higher than for some cards, at 15.9 percent, but because I usually pay it off each month, that doesn't matter. (If I am paying for something big like a vacation, I usually have all or almost all the money saved up, so I just pay with the card and then transfer the money into the credit card account.) Then two or three times a year, I have enough points to redeem a $50 or $100 gift certificate or rebate. It's quite handy. **Deb, 33**

WHICH CARD IS RIGHT FOR ME?

There are plenty of cards out in the marketplace, and finding one to suit your spending habits is a step toward being money savvy. Cardratings.com is an independent financial service research group that provides free information on a number of financial services, including credit cards. Here's a sample:

Delta SkyMiles Gold Credit Card (issued by American Express)

INTEREST   9.99% introductory rate, then 18.24%

CARD FEE $85 (waived first year or $30 if you have an
American Express charge card)

GRACE PERIOD 20 days

CARD PERKS   Reward program

Great if you pay off your balance each month and take advantage of the rewards program.

Citi Platinum Select Card

INTEREST   0% introductory rate, then 11.24% variable

CARD FEE   N/A

GRACE PERIOD 20 days

CARD PERKS   Travel and auto insurance, among others

Designed for those with good credit ratings.

Discover Platinum Card (issued by Morgan Stanley)

INTEREST   0% introductory rate, then 10.99% variable

CARD FEE   N/A

GRACE PERIOD 25 days

CARD PERKS   Reward program and cash rebates

Ideal if you have a good credit rating and are looking for a cash reward program.

Total Visa Card (issued by Plains Commerce Bank)

INTEREST   19.92% fixed

CARD FEE $48 annual fee (plus application fees; total first
year $296)

GRACE PERIOD 25 days

For those who have had problems in the past with paying off their credit card bills. Total Visa offers a card for those who need to establish credit again, or who have limited credit. It's a high price to pay in interest rate, but if you pay off your debts each month you have the ability to reestablish your credit rating.

AT&T Universal Platinum Credit Card

INTEREST   0% introductory rate, then 11.75% variable

CARD FEE   N/A

GRACE PERIOD 25 days

CARD PERKS   Good honeymoon rate for the first 12 months, and reasonably good thereafter. This low-rate credit card is ideal for those who have an excellent credit rating.

For other options, check out www.cardratings.com.

OUT OF SIGHT, OUT OF MIND, OUT OF TROUBLE

To get out of trouble, remove the temptation to spend.

Your credit card is like most other things in life: if you don't have it, then you don't miss it. If you've decided that all you want to do is pay off your credit card bill, then you can cut up the card, knowing that you can always apply for another one. Alternatively, give the card to a trusted friend or family member until you have paid your debt.

And to make paying the debt easier, do what fashion-addict Michelle did, and apply for a bank loan to cover the full amount owed on all your cards, then pay off the loan.

SOME "NEVER-EVER-EVERS"

Never take up an unsolicited offer to extend your credit card limit, particularly if you are having difficulty paying off the full amount each month, no matter how much the bank encourages you with gracious comments. For example, "As a long-standing loyal customer, we are offering you an increase on your limit." Yeah, right. Tear up the offer immediately.

Never take out a new credit card and pay off the old one with it—unless you can be guaranteed a very low interest rate for the first year to give you time to pay it off. And never ever unload monies between existing credit cards, withdrawing money on one to pay another. If you do, you are moving into very dangerous territory.

Avoid withdrawing cash from your credit card. The interest is charged immediately (even if your card offers interest-free days on goods purchased) and can quickly hike up your interest payments each month.

Steer clear of credit card merchants trying to entice you with offers, unless you're credit card savvy, like Kay:

I decided I would take up an offer on an in-store credit card of a 10 percent discount on the first $1,000 I spent. So I used the credit card to buy a few items, taking advantage of the discount. When the bill arrived, I paid off the debt and then canceled my card. **Kay, 33**

TIPS TO KEEP TRACK OF YOUR CREDIT CARD DEBT

- Jot down the amount of your purchases in an organizer or diary. At the end of each month, add up the figures so you're not waiting until the bill arrives to find out what you need to pay. Or check your statements online each week to keep track of your spending.
- Check your statements carefully. Make sure there are no surprises or overcharged amounts on your bill.
- Keep your credit balances low and pay your bills on time. One too many missed payments could knock 100 points off your FICO score.
- Don't increase your limit.
- To find out if your credit card matches the benefits of others available and to help you find a credit card to suit your lifestyle, you can visit www.cardratings.com.
- For information on credit cards, visit www.creditinfocenter.com. If your bills are out of control, visit the Association of Independent Consumer Credit Counseling Agencies (www.aiccca.org), a nonprofit counseling service.

$550

$355

CHAPTER FIVE

THE SEALED SECTION

There are some things that every savvy girl needs to know that really don't come up in polite conversation. Time for the hard facts.

MONEY, THE ROMANCE-WRECKER

Ah, falling in love. The swooning infatuation. You've met the man of your dreams, and everything is going according to plan—until you discover your ideas about money are completely different. Unfortunately, money is right up there at the top of the list of reasons relationships break up.

You may remember in chapter 3, Julie noted that she and her boyfriend have the same money beliefs, and this helps makes their relationship smooth. I'd go further than this, in fact a lot further. Money compatibility is crucial in a relationship.

Luckily, Julie has found her match. But what if you're on the opposite end of the scale from your partner—he's a tightwad and you're the last of the big spenders, or the other way around? If you don't deal with the differences early on, somewhere down the line you will have problems.

It is possible for such a relationship to work, but only if you're upfront about it and talk through your feelings, then reach an agreement about who pays for what, particularly if you are living together and paying bills together.

Sure, discussing finances with your partner can be tricky. It raises a whole host of sensitive issues, such as whether the person who earns more money has more say in financial matters. But ignoring it will lead to even trickier questions like who gets the sofa when you split up?

One savvy suggestion is to have three different bank accounts: one account for each of you and a joint account. The joint account covers rent or mortgage, household expenses, groceries, and other bills you split. You will need to agree on a percentage to take out of your salary each month to keep the joint account topped off. If you do it on a percentage basis, then you are both contributing what you can, regardless of who earns more. You may, for instance, choose to deposit 60 percent of your salary; the remaining money you can use for your individual expenses, such as credit cards, entertainment, or even investing.

Sexually transmitted debt

Everyone hopes that their relationship will last. But to protect yourself, you have to remain financially savvy. The sad fact is that romance doesn't always work out. Just look around at some of the people in your own circle—friends and family members—or think about your own past relationships. We need to be able to pick up the pieces if we find ourselves on our own.

What can you do?

Generally speaking, it's a good idea to know what's happening with your joint finances and to keep some financial independence within the relationship. You might feel at first that you are being disloyal by having your own savings account; you may worry that it looks as though you don't trust your partner. But that's the wrong way to look at it. You want the best for each other, right? Well, this is the best way to ensure financial security for both of you. When you're celebrating your golden wedding anniversary, you'll be glad you took care of the basics early on.

If you don't give yourself this level of security and something does somehow go wrong, you could end up with something that can be every bit as devastating as a sexually transmitted disease: sexually transmitted debt. This is when you are left with all his debts as well as yours after a breakup. You may discover unpaid bills that had been hidden from you or, in a worst-case scenario, your ex has suddenly disappeared, leaving you responsible for massive debts you weren't aware existed.

No matter what your age or circumstances, anyone who doesn't take precautions can fall victim to a partner's debt, just like Melissa did.

Eight years ago, I met the man of my dreams—or so I thought. I was 24 years old, and he was 20. Around this time, my career really took off. I was working in the hotel industry and needed to travel a lot. I earned a good salary; in fact, I was the primary earner when we decided to move in together. He was those few years younger than me, and I was a little concerned by this, but at the time he appeared mature for his age.

He had just started a full-time job, so I thought we could move in together and share the costs. Previously, he was living with his family and I was renting on my own, so it made sense.

Whoever said love is blind got it right. Even though he was earning, he continually complained that he had no money. I thought his money was going into his car, but I later discovered when I was away traveling for work, he was spending his money on going to clubs and doing drugs.

I had always been good with money and had very little on my credit cards. I paid all our bills. I even paid for his airfare so he could meet me on my work assignments abroad. How stupid was I? But he always said he would pay me back. And I was devoted to the relationship, so I thought it would work out in the end.

For our fourth anniversary, I paid the fares for us to take a short vacation. I ended up paying for everything. By now it was a habit. At the same time I applied for another credit card. I loved him so much that I thought we would be together forever. The thought of us breaking up never entered my mind. I did think of the money he owed me from over the years, but as stupid as it sounds, I let it pass because I thought we would never part, that we would get married. Not long after that, I discovered he was having an affair.

I bought him so much over the five years we were together. I gave him money all the time. Looking back now, after all the hurt and pain, I can see that it was partly my doing. I just kept applying for credit cards. They were so easy to obtain that after five years I had five credit cards plus loans covering the new furniture I bought when we moved in together. In total, I had $20,000 of debt.

My God, even as I tell this story again, I still can't believe how stupid I was. I'm a generous person, and even when he was short of money and I knew he was hanging out with the wrong crowd and doing drugs, I didn't want to abandon him. I tried to help, even when he was fired from two jobs. Even his own family told me not to give him any more money.

It was also hard to tell my family. Like I said earlier, I was always good with money and people used to ask me for loans. Now it was my turn. But once I told my family and friends, they were so supportive. They encouraged me along the way and helped keep me on track with my payments.

That was four years ago. Today I am much wiser, and in my mind, I know nothing is forever. The debt is almost paid off. I went to the bank, and thankfully they gave me a loan of $22,000. I paid off all my cards and closed them all. The interest payments alone were killing me—I couldn't keep up.

I am almost there now. One more year, and I will be free of debt and the bad memories of that relationship. Now I have a good job, and I put $500 every two weeks into clearing my debt—I have it automatically deducted.

It has been a hard road, but I am getting there, and the most important thing is that I'm happy and can sleep at night.

Now I have no credit cards, just a loan that will be gone in one year. Then I can concentrate on buying a condo. It's amazing how one person caused so much turmoil in my life, but I am also to blame. **Melissa, 33**

I've known Melissa for a long time, and she's right when she says she was always good with money. If it happened to her, it can happen to anyone who is trusting and too much in love to be suspicious.

It can certainly happen to older and wiser heads, too. At the launch of my first book, a woman approached me to tell me at the age of 65 she had finally found the courage to start investing. What led to her taking control of her finances was the death of her husband. During their time together he had always taken care of the bills—or so she thought. Only after he died did she discover they had a number of outstanding debts, amounting to thousands of dollars.

It came as a shock to her, but she had to deal with it. The first thing she did was approach her bank and explain the situation. Then she went about downsizing her house and car. With the money left over, she paid off the debt, and for the first time started to think about investing. When I met her she had started an investment club and was feeling in control. This just goes to show that it's never too late.

A safeguard against sexually transmitted debt

Keep your credit cards in your name only and do not sign or guarantee another person's loan or credit card. If you do and that person is unable to pay his or her bills, the credit provider will come after you, because by acting as a guarantor, you have made yourself fully responsible to pay the entire debt.

The prenup

Prenuptial agreements are no longer just for the rich and famous. Anyone who has ever been through a separation and lost a lot of money in the process would agree with the benefits of having a prenuptial agreement.

If you think the divorce and family law courts will favor women after a breakup, then you are kidding yourself. Men have long argued that they have been given a raw deal in the past, and unfortunately, this is probably true. The divorce laws vary from state to state. To find out what you can expect, it's worth visiting www.divorcelawinfo.com. It's a comphrehensive site with plenty of valuable resources and links.

The purpose of a prenuptial agreement is to protect the assets you bring into a relationship, particularly if you have more than your partner. Here's Carol's story:

I was married for nine years before we separated. My ex-husband and I had built up a very successful business, and when we split, I was determined to look after the assets I had gained during our marriage.

I wasn't looking for another relationship, particularly after a messy divorce. Unfortunately, when there is a lot of money at stake, it tends to be that way. I wanted to try to get back to a normal life with our three children.

I met my second husband quite by accident. He worked at my local bank, and we started seeing each other. After a year we decided to move in together. I had a lot more assets than he did, and we decided he would move into my house, as it was much larger than his apartment.

Perhaps it was because he was in the finance industry that he was very understanding when I talked to him about our finances. Mainly because I had a lot more to lose than he did, I wanted to make sure my assets and my children were protected should we go our separate ways.

We put everything in writing. Basically, if we break up we keep everything that we brought to the relationship. The things we accumulate together we would split according to who wanted it more, or who paid for it. He was really great about the whole thing. I guess that's another reason why we ended up getting married. **Carol, 36**

Legal advice

The American Bar Association Web site (www.abanet.org) is excellent and comprehensive, and will guide you to a list of resources in your state. Most legal issues are regulated by the law in the state where you live or where the problem occurred.

Click on "Public Resources," then go to "Consumers' Guide for Legal Help." From there, you can select the state where you live.

COVER YOUR GREATEST ASSET

Invincible, that's what you are, right? You have the freedom to come and go. Your career funds the lifestyle you have become accustomed to. Friends and family are always behind you. Life is looking pretty rosy, until . . .

It's breast cancer awareness month, and you decide to heed the message and do the right thing, so you visit your doctor for a breast examination.

Your doctor begins the examination, and stops suddenly. Your heart stops too, then accelerates as she recommends you have a mammogram as soon as possible. The unthinkable happens and a lump is detected; in an instant, life has changed. You need time off work. Surgery, chemotherapy, and recovery are now the priorities in your life.

We know it is a tough battle fighting a disease like cancer, but if you are struggling to make ends meet, the impact is so much worse. How are you going to cope?

The above events really happened to two good friends of mine. Luckily, they both had a disability income—a protection insurance plan that helped them through.

If you imagine it won't happen to you, stop and think for a minute. Both my friends were at the peak of their careers and were fit and seemingly healthy. Just look around at your friends and colleagues. You probably know someone who has had a life-threatening illness or other major health scare. Even the rich and talented are at risk: Anastacia, Sheryl Crow, Sharon Osbourne, and Olivia Newton-John are women who have found themselves battling life-threatening diseases, taking time out of their careers to recover.

Any number of illnesses or injuries can stop you in your tracks. Statistics suggest that half of working Americans will have a minimum of three months off work at some point due to an illness. Women in particular need to come to terms with this reality, particularly when they are helping to support children or are the sole breadwinner.

Imagine being struck down by a serious illness when you're by yourself with a mortgage. It happened to Penny:

I was going through a difficult time, and I had been under a fair amount of stress at work. There were a lot of deadlines to meet, and the pressure had been building up. I started to notice that I was getting sick often and had to take a few days off work.

One day I was walking along the street, and my legs gave out from under me. This was the beginning of a nightmare that has been with me for the past two years. I could not get up and sat on the sidewalk for some time. I then called a friend, who came immediately and took me straight to the medical center.

I notified my employer and they were really understanding and supportive, but what followed were months and months of medical tests. At one stage I was wheelchair-bound and I thought I was never going to walk again. I was so worried about my job and how I was going to survive. I had a mortgage, but luckily I had taken out income-protection insurance when I started my job. I work in the finance industry, and I guess I'm more aware of what coverage is available than most people. I have both disability income-protection insurance and life insurance.

The insurance means that if I become temporarily or permanently disabled, I'll get some benefit from my insurer.

Not for one minute did I think I would ever really need this insurance, certainly not so soon. I'm only 33 years old. I just got it because now that I have a mortgage, I do tend to worry a little more, plus I'm on my own. I'm conscious that I don't have anyone to fall back on.

The killer with my insurance policy was I had a 90-day waiting period before I got any money. But luckily I had some savings put aside, so I could survive on this money before the policy finally kicked in and my payment came through. It has been a lifesaver. I don't know what I would have done or how I would have survived without it. Almost a year after my initial collapse, they discovered I have a muscular disease, which continues to plague me.

I have returned to work now. I started with three short days a week, and now I'm almost back to full time. I can't do the things I used to do, like run or walk too far, and I do have relapses. Sometimes I can't get up out of bed from the muscle pain. I'm limited, but at least I was able to have time to recover, keep my job, and pay my bills, thanks to my disability income-protection insurance. **Penny, 33**

What to look for in disability income-protection insurance

Income-protection policies are generally offered by life and health insurance companies. If your employer doesn't offer this coverage, you can set it up for yourself. Make sure you are being covered for the work you perform. Define your income-producing duties. Ask yourself, are there any illnesses that you are not covered for? Make sure you receive this information in writing, and find out how long the waiting period is, for example, 90 days before you receive a payment.

Most policies should be able to provide you with an ongoing income. The income replacement level will vary depending on the policy you select. Most income-replacement levels cover between 60 and 100 percent of your income. Before you purchase your policy, select the income replacement level that is most suitable for your situation.

As your salary increases, check that your payments and projected payouts also increase.

If you aren't working full-time, check that your company will cover you—some policies don't cover part-time workers.

For more information or to help you estimate the cost of your premium, visit www.healthinsurancesavings.com; Northwestern Mutual Life, www.nmfn.com; or UNUM Provident, www.unumprovident.com.

Bear in mind that if you receive the disability benefit through your employer, it can be paid without affecting your income tax rate. However, should you then need to avail yourself of the benefit, the income will be taxable to you.

If you buy disability insurance on your own, you pay for it with "after tax" dollars. In this case, however, should you need to avail yourself of the benefits from the policy, they are paid tax free.

If you have a complaint about insurance, contact the North American Securities Administrators Association at www.nasaa.org.

DO YOU HAVE MILLIONAIRE CHARACTERISTICS?

Ever wanted to know what makes a millionaire and how they succeed? Author Thomas Stanley interviewed more than 300 ordinary women who became self-made millionaires for his book, *Millionaire Women Next Door*. He identified some characteristics they had in common. Check to see if you share them.

I. Perseverance. Whatever ideas the women had, they persevered, no matter what anyone said and regardless of what happened. For anyone who is in the process of starting her own business, perseverance is the number-one characteristic needed. Look at your favorite Olympic athlete if you need an inspiration boost: would they be where they are today if they gave up after each bad training session or race they lost? You can accept no boundaries if you wish to succeed. You must believe you can do it.

2. They receive tremendous satisfaction out of owning a business, achieving, learning, and making other people happy. And in many cases, this substitutes for high consumption and spending. The feeling of achievement you get when all your hard years of study pay off on graduation day, or when you land a great job or win someone's business you've put yourself on the line for, is one you simply can't match by accumulating possessions or partying. You can't put a price on that feeling.

3. They were not all gifted, the smartest people among their peers, or even given much of a start in life. Oprah Winfrey came from humble beginnings, but this didn't stop her from becoming the hottest woman on TV. Her passion and devotion to delivering the news and covering issues important to women—and men—has made her one of the wealthiest people in the United States.

4. Even after they made millions, they were still frugal with money and continued to live within their means. Some of the women still use discount coupons and shop at bulk discount stores. This is understandable if you started with nothing and then made a lot of money. If you've done it the hard way,

it's easy to remember what it was like to struggle financially. And a true bargain is still a bargain, no matter how much money you have.

5. More than 20 percent of the millionaire women interviewed were originally teachers. This makes sense, because teachers usually need to be well disciplined and intelligent. Also, they take the initiative and are usually very frugal—they have to be, since they are underpaid and their schools are usually underfunded. I take my hat off to teachers.

6. They were in the right profession to make the most of opportunities. Professions that lend themselves to young women becoming moguls are real estate, recruitment, business management, and child-care proprietorship.

YOUR BIGGEST HIDDEN ASSET

You could probably write a page-long list of your assets without hitting on one that is vital, but the one that is often forgotten is your pension. If you have done nothing in regard to investing or even putting money aside for a rainy day, then your pension or 401K will be all you have to fall back on—provided you've taken one out in the first place.

It's hard to imagine or even take an interest in your pension when you are in your 20s, but things really change when you hit your late 30s and 40s. You begin to wonder,

"Will I have enough to retire on?" and "Have I contributed enough?" Jobs may become more precarious as you get older. Also, it's worth understanding that the biggest slice of the American population, the baby boomers (born between 1946 and 1964), are nearing retirement. They'll be expecting large payouts from Social Security, putting pressure on and draining future cash reserves.

U.S. companies that do offer pension plans are on the decline. Although these are guaranteed at a federal level by the Pension Guarantee Board, there is a slight problem: the board is close to bankruptcy! With this in mind, you're probably getting the drift of the importance of setting up your own retirement fund.

One of the benefits of an employer retirement fund, the 401K, is that most employers will often match the amount you contribute, up to around 3 percent, sometimes more. These are voluntary, but if you arrange to have your contribution taken out of your salary before you get your hands on the money, you'll hardly notice the difference. When you come to retire, you'll be so glad that you made the contributions. Karen is in her late 30s and, like many women, wishes she had started earlier.

I've had a number of jobs over the years, and as a result I now have three plans, which I'll consolidate into my current plan. One is a high-risk fund returning 13.26 percent per annum, and the low risk is 7.91 percent. I only have about $13,000 in one fund and $6,000 in the other. I just started the third account when I changed jobs last May. I elected what percentage of my wage I wanted to contribute. My employer matches with 50 cents on every dollar contributed up to 6 percent of my wage, so if I contribute less than 6 percent I'm actually leaving money on the table, so to speak. My last employer had a 401K plan but didn't have an employer matching plan like my current one. I feel, like most people, that I waited too long to start a retirement fund. But when I was younger, I didn't know anyone who thought about doing it in their 20s or 30s. Now I wish I had contributed more when I was younger.

I have no idea what they will amount to when I retire. I may have to rely on Social Security as my main source of retirement money if the system doesn't go bust before then. I know we have a problem in the next five to ten years as the largest group of Americans all reach retirement age, leaving a mounting burden on the remaining workforce. They've already pushed back the retirement age for my generation to 67 instead of 65.

Americans just can't rely on a government pension. If I don't have enough to retire on, I'm convinced I'll have to move to Mexico or Central America. It's a little scary when I look to the future. **Karen, 39**

Why you should think about additional contributions

Women in particular are more likely to be out of the workforce for periods at a time, having children. When women return to work, our earnings are often reduced because we choose to work part-time or end up working on contract, with no retirement income. We often miss out this way in comparison to men. Unfortunately, many

Americans are totally unprepared for retirement and end up working, even if part-time, well into their 70s. Only 20 percent of the baby boomers who are nearing retirement will be financially savvy by the time they retire.

While you are young and earning solidly, it's definitely worth considering putting away a little extra, particularly if you may take time out of the workforce later.

If you do not have access to a government or corporate retirement program, why not set up your own retirement fund or IRA (individual retirement fund)? This can be done before taxes to a limited amount and after taxes—Roth 401K—to a larger amount. A Roth 401K operates like a retirement fund. You get no deduction when the money goes in, but you'll have a huge advantage later because you are building an account in which earnings will be permanently tax-free. You'll find lots of information on the following Web sites:

money.cnn.com/pf/retirement/
moneycentral.msn.com/retire/home.asp
finance.yahoo.com/retirement
smartmoney.com/retirement

How much do I need to retire on?

Retirement seems such a long way away. But think about it for a minute: how much would you need to live on? Of course, the ideal amount depends on many things, but mostly it's about the lifestyle you want.

The figures below give you an indication of the size of the lump sum you will need to have when you retire to generate the annual income you want. (It's calculated on a lump sum superannuation payout and earnings of around 6 to 7 percent a year.)

$330,000 will generate $20,000 a year.
$480,000 will generate $30,000 a year.
$820,000 will generate $50,000 a year.
$1,000,000 will generate $60,000 a year.

If you're looking at these figures and saying, "There's no way I could live off $20,000 or even $30,000," all of a sudden retirement money issues start to become more real, even though it won't happen for decades. This is the best time in your life to do something about it—when you're 50, you'll never be able to catch up. Start by adding more voluntary amounts to your pension fund, or at least keep up your minimum contributions to your 401K plan while you are working. If you change jobs, don't forget to transfer or roll over your plan to your new company—that way you'll maintain your retirement fund's consistent earnings.

Bear in mind, when they retire most people will own their home and car. Their kids should be off their hands. But the bills still come in, and you do not want to be trying to live on just Social Security, trust me.

Where to go to find out your entitlements

The Social Security Administration at www.socialsecurity.gov will help you figure out what your retirement income is likely to be by using the benefits calculator. You can try out various scenarios, including a quick or detailed calculation, to find out how much you need to save to achieve the final retirement income you want.

And if you have lost track of your pension plan (maybe because you have bits and pieces in different accounts from previous jobs but don't know where to find them), give the Social Security Administration office a call at (800) 772-1213.

While we're on the subject of lost money, it is estimated that nine in ten Americans are owed cash, which sits unclaimed each year. To find unclaimed royalties, commissions, trust account funds, uncollected goods, unpresented checks, and salary, you can go to www.yourunclaimedmoney.org, or www.cashunclaimed.com. I know it's a long shot, but if you happen to be one of those people, then the next round of cocktails is on you!

CHAPTER SIX

YOUR MONEY HOROSCOPE

Ever wondered what the stars say about you and your money habits? Astrologer Kelly Surtees takes a close look at what your star sign reveals about your money personality. Are you indecisive or diligent when it comes to handling your finances? What traps do you have to watch out for? And what are the financial strengths you may not even know you have?

ARIES: CONFIDENT AND CRAVES INSTANT GRATIFICATION
March 21–April 19

By nature, this Mars-ruled sign is impulsive, courageous, impassioned, and inspired. Aries individuals tend to act first, then think later. They are confident about taking the initiative.

The "I want it now" drive of Aries translates to a desire for instant gratification, and with credit card at the ready, it's all too easy. The first step for you, Aries, might be to leave the credit card at home (remember—out of sight, out of mind).

The courage Aries is known for gives you strength and confidence to make changes and take charge regarding investments. While other signs may endlessly deliberate about the merits, or lack thereof, of certain investment opportunities, you possess an innate understanding that the only true way to find out what works or doesn't work is to give it a try. Your inspiration and dreams for something more than what you have today means you are happy to take a loss. You would rather have given something a shot than done nothing at all.

Your short attention span and responsive nature may, however, see you chopping and changing between investment products or stocks more often than is wise. Embracing the lesson of patience regarding investments will be your most valuable investment decision.

TAURUS: HAPPIEST SURROUNDED
BY BEAUTIFUL THINGS
April 20–May 20

Ruled by Venus, you are easily enticed into spending money on beautiful things, body treatments, clothes, and decorations for the home. Anything that helps make you or your space prettier is an easy sell as far as you're concerned.

Taurus is known as one of the money signs, for as much as you spend, you are also quite good at making money (Phew!). The pleasurable things in life are worth spending money on, according to you. Generally, big expenditures are easily handled by your steady earth energy. As a fixed sign, you find it easy to commit long term to financial plans. Finding the freedom within your big plans for a little retail therapy here and there helps you maintain control.

The Taurus energy is associated with the farming cycle— building each year on what you have achieved in the previous one. This mentality is great when applied to your savings plan. You understand that saving even a little today makes for a lot tomorrow. Money seems to flow around you—plenty coming in and going out. The trick for you is to siphon a consistent amount into long-term financial investments.

With your slow and steady nature, the time required to make a financial plan bear fruit is usually not a barrier. Coming to grips with the reality that a mortgage or savings plan doesn't mean no shopping (just less) is a big step toward financial independence for you!

GEMINI: INDECISIVE AND A WORRIER

May 21–June 21

Easily influenced and quick to change, Geminis have a hard time settling on the idea of setting up a financial plan, let alone deciding what investment avenues to follow. Your tendency to worry and feed yourself excessive amounts of information is best put to rest by employing a trusted financial adviser or planner.

A view of the bigger picture of your overall plan will keep you focused on moving forward instead of getting caught up in today's current favorite investment option. Unless you are specifically educated in the field of money management, you will do well to have a professional provide information for key decisions.

Your constant indecision about which choice to make could mean you sometimes miss opportunities. Your natural curiosity can run amok and see your investments spread too thinly across a wide range of options. Obtaining some professional advice will help you narrow down your investment scope while still maintaining some diversity. Your natural desire for different interests shows that you are comfortable with the concept of diversifying and picking appropriate investment options for your personal situation.

CANCER: SWAYED BY EMOTIONS
AND TAKES SMALL RISKS

June 22–July 22

As a sign concerned with protection, you will naturally be looking for safer or lower-risk investments to protect your underlying capital. High-risk or speculative choices will have you feeling out of your depth. Finding investment choices that have a lower risk will leave you feeling safe and in control.

In money management, as in life, rewards can sometimes only be gained by taking at least a small amount of risk. Your confidence and ability to extend yourself in the financial world is linked to your confidence and your ability to take risks. You are a sign easily swayed by emotions. Particularly when it comes to the all-important home purchase, you will need to take care that your emotions don't interfere with your budget. Having a trusted friend or adviser to help keep you focused on the financial aspect of a decision is important.

Ruled by the moon, your feelings ebb and flow like the tides, and separating emotions from money-related decisions will be a key factor on your journey to financial independence. Family may have a big influence on your money beliefs. Just remember, even though they are family members, their situations will differ from yours.

LEO: A SHOW-OFF WHO
LOVES MATERIAL OBJECTS
July 23–August 22

As a proud individual, you like to surround yourself with material objects that you can show off. This can lead to a tendency to overspend on some of the more discretionary items like clothing, your home, a car, and jewelry. With self-esteem so linked to what others think of your appearance, your budget can blow out at the mere mention of an important function or social event.

Disconnecting from what others think about how you dress, the car you drive, or where you live will be a key step in you curbing some of your excessive spending. While financial investments are nowhere near as glam as a prestige car or designer handbag, they will set you up for a stronger platform to treat yourself in the years to come.

Like your fellow fixed signs Taurus, Scorpio, and Aquarius, you tend to overthink or overplan. Sometimes this leads to you missing key investments, because you feel like you need even more information. Allow the fiery energy running through your veins to take charge and make a decision. Your natural leadership skills mean you won't feel like you have to wait until all your friends get into the housing market or investment field before you do—instead of trying to set trends in the glamour stakes, why not lead the way into the investment world?

VIRGO: EXCESSIVELY ANALYTICAL, AND MAY MISS THE BIG PICTURE
August 23–September 22

Meticulous and famously detail-oriented, you are extraordinarily well ordered. Your ability to set up systems and run processes is second to none in the zodiac and, when applied to your bank balance, will be a great gift. However, one trap that many Virgos fall into is the "failure to see the forest for the trees" syndrome, where the small details become such a focus that you forget to keep sight of the bigger picture.

Keeping an eye on an ultimate long-term goal will help prevent you from excessively analyzing the little steps that you are taking to get there. Sometimes life will distract you from where you are going, and small adaptations need to be made in the realm of the everyday. But if you are able to keep moving toward a final goal, the worry that plagues you so often will dissipate a little.

You understand that information-gathering and research is necessary but doesn't need to be taken to extremes. Your willingness to apply your keen planning and organizational skills to your money management is a measure of how successful you will be on the road to financial independence.

LIBRA: INDECISIVE AND GENTLE BY NATURE
September 23–October 22

The biggest financial challenge facing you is the indecisiveness that is known to plague those born under your sign. The need to weigh out options from all angles sometimes means you miss the action, because come deadline day, you're still debating the pros and cons.

Your gentle nature means that you sometimes lack the assertiveness to push yourself ahead of the pack in the financial world. Your strong desire for fairness is of no use when it comes to money management, since not everyone is a winner in this game. Allowing yourself to succeed where others may not will be a big step forward for you. It is okay to achieve on your own—don't be held back waiting for everyone else to get their act together.

What may work very effectively for you, Libra, is to get together with an investment group or organization that will allow you to surround yourself with like-minded people and encourage you to make decisions and move forward to your goal of financial freedom.

SCORPIO: STUBBORN BUT MONEY SAVVY
October 23–November 21

You are commonly referred to as the sun sign with the most canny money-managing skills. Your ability to work effectively with the resources you have at any point means you are constantly looking ahead financially. Money is one subject with which you are comfortable.

You are quick to recognize there is a certain amount of power and freedom that comes from having a solid financial base. What may hold you back is your stubborn, fixed nature that wants to explore all possibilities before acting.

Your tenaciousness when it comes to thoroughly researching investments will serve you well with the large and slower-paced investment styles. Your ability to take a long-term view means that you are happy to miss out on small gains today in the hope of larger gains down the road. You may be rather suspicious of any short-term, flavor-of-the-month investment vehicles that come your way, which is not necessarily a bad thing.

Your nature is more comfortable with big-scale, future-oriented investments.

SAGITTARIUS: A "DON'T FENCE ME IN" ATTITUDE REQUIRES A SAVINGS PLAN
November 22–December 21

Happy-go-lucky and freedom-loving, you are often more concerned about where and when the next adventure will start. Money only comes into the equation as a means to an end. Motivating yourself through travel or study goals will help you stick to a more mundane savings plan.

Ruled by Jupiter, planet of optimism, you have little desire to plan much for the future on any level, preferring to trust that you will always land on your feet. And in many areas of life, you will. However, a solid financial platform doesn't fall from the sky (unless, of course, you have some aging relatives ready to leave their fortune to you!). Getting your head around the fact that putting something away today means more travel or freedom in the future will get you started. Realizing that a mortgage is a step toward that extended overseas trip (you can always rent out the property) and not a ball and chain weighing you down is a good beginning. Look for investments that won't curb your spontaneous lifestyle too much today but allow you to put money away for an even more freedom-filled tomorrow.

CAPRICORN: PRACTICAL AND DILIGENT, YOU TAKE THE LONGER-TERM VIEW WITH SAVINGS
December 22–January 19

Known for your steady and practical nature, you always have your eye on your current financial status. You take a longer-term view than most and have an innate awareness that money doesn't grow on trees. Instead, it must come from a little diligence and saving.

With your cautious—and at times reserved—nature, you will be looking for more traditional styles of investment. Perhaps investment options that worked for your parents, those tried-and-true moneymakers like real estate, are where you are likely to be comfortable putting your money. The new investment products may confuse you a little, but if you apply your dogged research capabilities to reading the fine print, you may find these modern investment products have something to offer. If you choose to apply your management and organizational abilities to your finances, you will be well on the way to financial freedom.

A financial plan is similar to a business plan, and if you add it to your to-do list, you'll find yourself making a priority of managing your money.

AQUARIUS: AHEAD OF THE REST
WHEN IT COMES TO MONEY
January 20–February 18

You are known for your ahead-of-the-times ideas, and you may struggle to understand where the rest of us are at in terms of money management. Your concepts usually go way ahead of what is available today, as the mass only moves at the speed of the slowest mind.

What you will need to do in order to build financial security for yourself is stop trying to force everyone else to move at your pace and instead look for innovative ways to work around what is currently available in the investment world. Your high level of intelligence would better be put to use on humanitarian projects or cutting-edge technology, as the mundane everyday demands of life lack the spark to keep you interested for long. However, once you set your mind on something, you are likely to see it through.

Find ways of making investing inventive, and you will see your interest and commitment levels rise. You will benefit greatly from a trusted adviser who will integrate some of your more left-field ideas into today's investment options.

PISCES: DREAMY, YOU STRUGGLE WITH POSSESSIONS AND MATERIAL THINGS
February 19—March 20

Your dreamy nature is not the best for meeting the demands of money management. However, one thing that is often overlooked when traditionalists describe your sign is the innate ability Pisceans have for working with power.

In our modern society, money very much equals power, and you have an inner ability to attract just what is necessary to you at the right time financially. Like your fellow Jupiter-ruled Sagittarians, you tend not to plan for the future, trusting it will take care of itself.

Pisceans really struggle with possessions, so you lack the desire for buying things that motivates so many people toward financial freedom.

What your Piscean mind needs to grasp is that money and a solid financial base also equal freedom—something you long for deeply. With some money behind you, you could travel on a whim or take a sabbatical from work to pursue more spiritual or esoteric pursuits. You may need to employ an earthy advisor to keep you saving regularly, but keeping the ultimate goal of personal freedom in your mind will keep you moving on the path to financial independence.

Kelly Surtees is a professional astrologer who combines traditional and experiential techniques to bring astrology alive for each individual. For more information, visit www.kellysurtees.com.

CHAPTER SEVEN

THE GIRLS MAKE HEADWAY

In chapter 2, we discussed cutting back on some of the smaller expenses to save you thousands of dollars over the course of a year. Did you manage to find areas where you could cut back? If you have but you're still looking to save a bit extra, then here are some more ideas you can put into place right now.

As you've seen, the scale you're trying to save on doesn't matter—whether it's just trying to make ends meet or saving for the latest Jimmy Choo shoes, a vacation, a car, or even a property, you can begin to make these small changes without too much compromise. These stories show how easy it is and how great it will make you feel.

DAY-TO-DAY TIPS

I'm not a heavy smoker by any means, but I do like to smoke when I go out with my friends. I figured by cutting back on a packet of cigarettes a week, I was already saving $4, or close to $20 a month. I decided I wanted to give it up because I was scared I would want to have more and become addicted, and then it would cost me hundreds of dollars a year. I'm glad I quit before it got to that stage—not to mention the health side of things. **Louise, 24**

I try to buy clothing that doesn't need to be dry-cleaned. Not only am I saving the cost of dry-cleaning, I also don't have the hassle of remembering to drop them off and pick them up. **Josephine, 35**

When my partner and I decided it was time to stop paying rent and buy a place of our own, the first thing we did was download one of those budget planners you find on the Web. It was a great help, because we needed to find out where our money was going before we could find ways to cut back. **Juanita, 26**

I really believe that starting small is a good way to start saving. When I went through my bills, especially my phone bill, I saw that I was paying $5 a month to have call-waiting. I decided to get rid of this cost, because I figured if someone really needed to talk to me they would call back. It's a tiny amount, but still, there's $60 a year saved without me even noticing. The other thing I did was cut back on newspapers and magazines. I know it's not much, but I would spend around $25 a month on newspapers. What I do now is just get the Sunday paper, and I read the daily papers in our office. **Angela, 27**

I have had to move a number of times, and I find that each time I move I end up with a lot of stuff that I've bought or just accumulated. What I have done twice now is have a yard sale. The last one I had was with a friend who had just broken up with her boyfriend and she wanted to get rid of a lot of stuff and move into a smaller place. With two of us, we shared the advertising cost in the local paper and we pocketed around $300 each for the day's work. It's such a relief to get rid of stuff and not have to cart it into the new place. **Dianne, 35**

One thing I make sure of is having enough food in the house for the week. I will shop on the weekend and buy things like snack bars and enough bread to make sandwiches. I also buy things like Lean Cuisine meals for those nights when I don't feel like cooking. It's still cheaper than eating out or getting take-out. It just takes a little planning at first. Now I'm used to it, it's just second nature to make my lunch. I know I have saved hundreds of dollars over the last two years. I'm saving because I want to buy a condo. **Alana, 33**

I have money automatically taken out of my salary and put into a savings account. I never see it, so I don't miss it. **Pearl, 26**

Many years ago, I heard someone suggest that putting money aside in designated envelopes would help to pay bills. Basically, once you got paid you immediately put the money aside in a separate envelope for each bill that has to be paid for the month, before you have time to spend it. I thought this was a good idea but a bit too structured for me. What I do is have two jars and at the end of the week I take the loose change from my wallet and put this into the jars. One jar I have labeled "shoes," and the other is for going-out expenses. I'll put more away in the going-out expenses jar, only because I dip into it more than the shoe jar. I always need a new pair of great shoes each season, and the money I save in the jar just about covers the cost. **Alice, 33**

I really like the idea of taking the loose change from your wallet each week. It may seem minuscule, but over time it adds up. Many years ago I met a guy who'd done just that. Each week he put his loose change in a bottom drawer. When he discovered he was about to become a father, he decided to put the money into a savings account for his child's education. Without fail, each month for 20 years, he would put his monthly haul of change into the account. The money he saved plus the interest he earned on it was enough for him to pay for his son's education.

I used to spend a lot of money on clothes, but then I stopped. Mainly because my best friend moved overseas and shopping wasn't as much fun without her. I'm just not a brand person and could never spend $200 on a pair of shoes, but we used to visit thrift stores and markets together, and we both loved bargains. It's just not fun in the same way when she's not around. I've never saved so much, and now I'm planning to go overseas next year to meet up with her. **Tara, 26**

While it's a little drastic to send your friends overseas just to save you money, it may be worth considering the impact they have on your expenditures. Could your friends be a real part of the reason you're spending way too much on clothes?

PUTTING YOUR MONEY TO WORK

I found it amusing when someone called me an investor just because I told them that I had invested money in a managed fund. I hardly thought of myself that way, because you think of an investor as some guy doing deals in a big stockbroking firm or something. All I did was take $1,000 and put this into a managed fund and then add $100 each month. It was really easy, and I don't do anything, apart from checking the statement when it comes in the mail at the end of the financial year. **Chelsea, 29**

If you're still at the stage of struggling to keep on top of your bills, finding a lazy $100 to put away each month like Chelsea did might sound like a pipe dream. But you can get yourself into a position to do it, and it's definitely worthwhile.

If you put $100 a month into a managed fund earning, say, 6 percent interest a year, you would have $16,400 after ten years. That's $4,400 more than the $12,000 you actually put away, thanks to compound interest. It's one smart way of making your money work for you.

Here are some surefire strategies to help you find that $100 every month to stash away in a managed fund without compromising your lifestyle.

20 TIPS TO HELP GET YOU STARTED

1. Cut back on one coffee a day and only buy lunch three days a week, and you could save as much as $1,700 a year.

2. Don't forget that the matinee movie showings are generally cheaper. Try to grab an early afternoon movie and save a few dollars. Another place worth checking for discounts on movies and DVDs is Working Advantage (www.workingadvantage.com). Or purchase books that offer half-price coupons on entertainment at www.entertainment.com.

3. Start your own movie club. We all love the movies, so as well as buying discounted movie theater tickets, why not start a monthly DVD club? Use the same principles as a book or gourmet club, and share take-out while watching the movie. Ask everyone to chip in, and you'll pay around $10 for the night, instead of $30 for a movie and a meal out.

4. Start a money diary. All you need is one week. Write down every dime you spend. Once you see where all your money is going, then you can start to cut back. It's really simple but very effective.

5. If you are not a heavy cell phone user, choose a pay-as-you-go plan. Capped plans work best for heavy cell users.

6. Be particular about ATMs. Withdraw money only from your own bank's ATMs. Ten withdrawals from other banks' ATMs will cost at least $15 a month in fees.

7. Carry minimum cash in your wallet. That way, you won't be tempted to spend.

8. Take out your loose change at the end of each day and drop it in a piggy bank. You'll be surprised how much you can save with no noticeable impact on your spending.

9. Limit your credit card debt to a level you are able to pay off each month. And no matter how many times your bank encourages you to increase your limit, don't.

10. Get into the habit of walking. Save money that would otherwise go to public transportation and cabs, and get fit at the same time.

11. Start a gourmet or book club. You'll have a lot of fun and save a wad of cash. Designate one night each month for a chance to catch up and gossip with friends at one another's places.

12. Visit eBay and learn to shop online. If you buy wisely, you can save a heap: remember Maria and her $15 designer shoes from chapter 4.

13. Choose restaurants that let you bring your own wine. A little planning before your evening starts will mean painless savings, particularly if you are going with a large group where the alcohol can cost at least as much as the food bill or more.

14. Only buy what's on sale. Adopt this habit today, and you won't have to wait long to grab a bargain. You'd be crazy to pay retail price for anything!

15. Get on the e-mail list of your favorite designers, and you'll find out ahead of the general public when their sales are.

16. Opt for less flashy beauty products. Consumer surveys have repeatedly shown that the Nivea, Ponds, and Olay range offers the same benefits as the more glamorous brands, so don't be sucked in by the glossy ads—shop around and save.

17. Visit your local library if you're an avid reader. The books are up-to-date and free.

18. Don't forget Internet auctions. There are some good and reputable online auction sites (e.g., www.auctiondrop.com and www.foundvalue.com) where you can buy anything from new computer equipment to secondhand furniture. Remember to set yourself a limit before you place a bid—and stick to it.

19. Write down your goals. Put them somewhere prominent to remind you why you are saving. This could be in your wallet, or as a screen saver, or written down in your diary at the start of each week. Tell your friends and family so everyone can support you.

20. Make the most of things that are free. During the summer months, many parks have free outdoor movie screenings. Grab a few friends, take a picnic, and enjoy the night. Google your nearest park to find out when the next screening will be held.

Try at least five of these tips for one month and see how much you save. You'll soon be a convert.

CHAPTER EIGHT

CUTTING DOWN THE BIG TICKETS

Day to day, you're making a whole lot of small changes that are making a big difference. But what about those whopping great expenses like cars, weddings, and travel? By being savvy, you can save on these big-ticket expenses too.

A GIRL'S GOTTA HAVE WHEELS

Having your own car signals freedom. No more asking for rides from parents and friends. Or, worse still, after a great night out, being forced to stand on street corners trying to flag down a cab.

Did you know most women choose a car based on the influence of parents, friends, and boyfriends? For example, if your parents drove a Ford, you may be swayed to do the same. Then again, you may opt for something you think reflects more of your own personality: sporty and fun, like a Honda Civic. If you want something on the conservative side, you may prefer a classic sedan. Or something funky like a VW. If you're more eco-minded, a hybrid is perfect. The bottom line is, you need to pick a car that suits your lifestyle and budget.

But before we get to the nuts and bolts, what about the following must-haves in a girl's dream car of the future?

- The obvious—more mirrors, please
- Automatic lipstick applicator
- "Single male" detector. Detects the nearby males of your choice once you input your preferred stats: i.e., tall, dark, and handsome, with a red sports car
- Built-in steamer for pressing clothes
- Self-cleaning car, similar to a self-cleaning oven
- A portable hair dryer that runs off the cigarette lighter or, better still, a hair straightener (I know a girl who actually asks cab drivers if she can plug her straightener into the cab's cigarette-lighter socket to do her hair on the way.)
- Driver's seat massage feature
- Three sizes of cup holders for small/medium/large coffees (depending on how late you stayed up partying the night before)

- More color choices inside and outside of the car or, better yet, seat covers you can change at the flick of a switch to match your outfits
- More trunk space for all the shopping bags

Now, back to what's actually out there . . .

The consensus for how much you should pay for a secondhand car is about $8,000. This is enough to get you into some cool wheels and avoid a lemon. That's not to say you can't buy a good car for under $8,000. It will just take more work and research, and you will be looking at a car that is older and has more mileage.

While we love our wheels, there are ongoing expenses that you will need to consider each year. If you live in a city and work reasonably nearby, you may find that it is truly more economical for you to take cabs and use public transportation when you consider all the costs associated with owning a car.

When Amanda added it all up, she found that using public transportation was the only way to go. An environmentally conscious employer was a big contributing factor in her decision.

I actually estimated what a car would cost me. I found the cost was ridiculous when I compared it with public transportation costs. When I did the math, I included registration, gas, and general maintenance and saw it was going to cost around $50 to $70 a week! This is after I had paid for the car. These additional costs would be ongoing, so using public transportation was much cheaper. I'm a bit of an environmentalist as well, so I do believe in using public transportation. I live close to a major city, and generally getting around is fairly easy.

In my previous job I had a company car, and when I started this job with the local government I was entitled to a company car but I didn't take it, so they gave me an additional $5,000 a year as part of my salary package. My company is great because they are trying to encourage people to take public transportation. Another incentive was they would pay for half of my weekly travel ticket.

So I take cabs or public transportation to work. My employer also provides access to a number of company cars for meetings during the day. The only thing is, you don't take the car home at night. **Amanda, 26**

For Amanda, getting by without a car is easy, but what about the rest of us who rely on our wheels? Let's look at some of the costs associated with owning a car. The biggies are:

- Registration
- Auto insurance
- Gas
- Repairs and maintenance
- Parking fees and tolls

Registration

A new or used car requires registration, with fees typically running from $50 to more than $250. The cost to register your car will vary from state to state. Smaller and cheaper cars should attract lower registration charges.

You can contact the Department of Motor Vehicles in your state for an accurate cost. Visit www.usadmv.org and click on your state to find your local office.

Auto insurance

You're usually required by law to have this. It can be costly, but there are some great sites on the Web that offer reduced premiums. They also offer flexible payment plans. Before you commit to your insurer, one site definitely worth a visit is www.insweb.com. This site will help you find the best insurance in your state. It also has a terrific section on "The top five ways to save on your auto insurance." For example, most insurances companies offer a good-driver discount to those who have not had an accident in the past three to five years. You can also get discounts if you're a student.

The Web site www.findinsurance.com gives you the opportunity to obtain five insurance company quotes at once, which is a simple way of deciding which policy is best for you.

Once you decide on an insurer, you can take advantage of easy payment options like monthly installments, rather than paying one large annual bill (but note that it usually costs more to pay in installments). In the past, my auto insurance was due in December and I found the cost on top of Christmas bills quite stressful. Now I opt to pay it twice a year, and that has taken the pressure off.

Liz found out how worthwhile it was to shop around:

I found a massive difference in costs for my auto insurance between different companies. I was amazed. I just thought I'd take a quick glance at it, because I figured they'd all be about the same. In the end, I spent 20 minutes on the Web site www.ambest.com to help compare automobile insurance companies. Then I spent about 40 minutes calling around to different companies, and it was so worth it.

I'm a late starter when it comes to driving—even though I'm 32, I only got my license 18 months ago. I've only been driving for six months, which makes insurance much more expensive, because I'm not entitled to the good-driver discounts, which can be as much as 20 percent. I was looking for two different kinds of insurance—first up, liability coverage. You need this to pay for any damage you cause to other people with your car.

I also wanted to find out about comprehensive insurance—if the car got stolen or damaged by fire, vandalism, earthquake, or whatever. I really didn't have a lot of money to buy the car in the first place, and I didn't want to go into debt over it because I have a monthly mortgage and want to keep up my payments, so I only spent $3,500 buying the car. (I did some research beforehand to make sure I got something reliable—especially important when you have to buy an older car—and it paid off. The car is really reliable.)

Anyway, the highest insurance quote was $1,588 a year, and the lowest was $800! Maybe the first company (one of the biggies) stays in business because people don't check out other options. But even $800 was too much for a $3,500 car. Then I found a company that offered discounts if I took out property insurance with them, so I saved a little there. Also, another bonus was if I had an accident, my rates would not go up. As I'm a new driver, I found this reassuring.

They gave me a quote, and it was a price I could live with. It covers me for damage I might do to other people's property, plus damage from fire, lightning, theft, and attempted theft. It cost me around $700 a year. I've opted to pay monthly installments of $60.

So I got most of what I need (although I do still get very nervous when earthquakes are predicted, because I don't have insurance for that), and I saved hundreds of dollars. What I learned from all this was to shop around and look beyond the big companies you see advertised on TV.
Liz, 32

Gas

Gas-rebate credit cards may be for you. If you use the card responsibly and pay off your balance in full each month, this can be a great way to save on gas. Several credit cards offer a 5 percent rebate on gas purchases, along with no annual fee. So at a price of $3 a gallon, you'll save 15 cents per gallon. The Citibank Dividend Platinum Select MasterCard is a popular option—you'll get a 5 percent rebate from your gas purchases, and you can use the gas station of your choice, as long as it's a stand-alone gas station (i.e., one that is not affiliated with Wal-Mart or another supermarket). Some large grocery stores or warehouse clubs also offer rebates on gas for their customers, but it's only around 1 or 2 percent. For more information, check out www.cardratings.com.

Repairs and maintenance

This one is a little tricky, and the best recommendation would be to ask your friends and family if they know a reputable mechanic. It is sad but true: if you're not careful you could end up paying for expenses that were really unnecessary, particularly if you're a young woman who is vulnerable and doesn't know anything about cars. But even couples can get caught out.

After saving $10,000 of their own money, Sally and her fiancé Robert bought a new car. They borrowed the extra $11,000 from a bank. They were also looking to buy a home and had shopped around and were happy with the lender. The agent offered them a good deal on the interest payments.

There is nothing like owning a new car, so they were ecstatic when the keys were handed over. They felt pressured into agreeing when the car salesperson said they must have the car serviced at his dealership, but because it was a new car they thought they wouldn't rack up any large expenses. The first and second time they had the car serviced, they were charged $200 a visit. On the third visit, they were charged $750 for a service on a car that was only 18 months old.

Note: When buying a new car, make sure you understand exactly what the warranty covers. Generally, a new car is covered for three to four years for mechanical failures. Some warranties even include routine maintenance.

I didn't speak to Robert for a week. I had said to him earlier that we were paying too much and found out that if I had taken it to a regular registered mechanic for a service, it would have been a fraction of the cost. **Sally, 32**

Don't forget, we women have great instincts, and if you feel uncomfortable or in any way patronized, just walk right out. Lisa says she wishes she'd done just that. After continual disappointment with her mechanic's nit-picking, she finally decided to take her business elsewhere:

I felt extremely ill at ease each time I took my car to a local mechanic. I decided that this would be the last time, as some of the charges were totally unnecessary. Get this—among other things, he said my license plate was "scratched and not straight"!

Every time I went, he would pick on things that I felt were unjustified. I started to ask my female friends if they knew a good mechanic. Sure enough, I got a recommendation from a friend and I'm so glad I made the change.

The new mechanic is very approachable and friendly, and I don't feel he is cheating me. He didn't even mention the scratch on my license plate! **Lisa, 31**

Parking and tolls

Many parking lots within shopping malls offer the first two hours free. Let's face it, no respectable girl is going to get her shopping done in less than two hours, so be prepared to pay the hourly fees thereafter. You're still far better to be in a parking lot than out on the street copping a hefty parking fine.

If you're going to land yourself parking fines, you may as well just save time and tear up your money before you leave home.

After considering all the expenses, if you're still in the market for a car, here's what to look for:

A car-buying checklist

- Never buy a car from a salesperson with a "trust me" attitude. Remember your instincts.
- Shop with a friend. A male friend would be ideal. (The world should have progressed by now for this not to be necessary but, sadly, it still is.)
- Depending on your job and your life outside of work, you could spend many hours a week in your car, so make sure you pick a car to suit your lifestyle.
- Safety is paramount—if possible, buy a car with the three As: airbags, ABS brakes, and air-conditioning (comfort's pretty important, too!).
- Take the car for a thorough test drive.
- Look out for rust or bad paint jobs.
- Avoid cars that are gas-guzzlers. If you don't, you'll find that gas quickly becomes a major expense in your weekly budget.
- Consider a hybrid car if you're worried about gas

prices increasing. Hybrid cars combine a gasoline engine with a battery-powered electric motor. They're good for the environment, because they use less gas and produce less pollution.

There are some great Web sites around designed to take care of some of the hard work. You'll find used car values, new car prices, and reviews of various models. Check out these sites:

- carfax.com
- money.cnn.com/autos
- carbargainsweekly.com
- Kelley Blue Book at www.kbb.com for fair pricing

Once you have found a car to your liking, have the vehicle inspected by your local automobile association, such as the American Automobile Association (www.aaa.com).

Or use the www.carfax.com Web site and expect to pay $19.99 for a single vehicle history report. This is not the time to skimp—the inspection report can save you from wasting thousands on a dud.

If you plan to borrow to buy a car, shop around to get the best deal on interest payments. Don't hesitate to apply to credit unions and building societies if they come out ahead, even if you're not already a customer.

Consider buying a car at an auction. I did this and saved more than $5,000 on the price of buying it privately. I did have my husband, who is good with cars, to give advice, which was very helpful. Generally, the auction center will offer a three-month warranty or guarantee free of charge. For extended warranties, a small fee would apply, depending on the source.

Make sure the car has its entire service history and logs. This will tell you whether it has been well maintained.

It sounds obvious, but when you're standing in front of a cute car with a check in your hand, you can forget the basics, so it's worth a reminder: if possible, avoid cars with high mileage.

THE CELL PHONE

Not for one minute am I going to suggest that you consider life without your cell phone. That would be like asking you to abandon one of your trusted friends. But if you've never really looked at how much yours is costing, you should. You could be paying much more than you need to.

For example, the time at which you make your calls could make all the difference. Some monthly plans have higher rates during the day and free evening and weekend calls. If you're not making the most of these times, then it's worth contacting your phone provider, just like Kelly did.

I was making a lot of calls at night, particularly as this was the only time I found I could catch up with my friends and family after work. I had a much cheaper talk time after 9 p.m., but I found this was a little late to make all my calls. I contacted my phone provider and spoke to a customer service representative. I explained that I didn't want to break my contract—I just wanted to make the most of my phone plan and have the cheaper talk time brought to 7 p.m. They agreed. I had to pay a $5 fee to upgrade, but it was worth it. **Kelly, 32**

Depending on your cell phone provider, there are deals available that are worth their weight in gold, particularly if you choose one that has, say, free talk time. Lily explains:

I'm not technically minded, and to be honest I only got a cell phone two years ago. I was really confused by some of the deals.

[Aren't we all! For an industry that is all about communicating, the information they put out is incredibly confusing.]

And some of my friends were saying I should sign up for a plan. But I didn't want to go on a plan and be hooked into something I didn't understand. In the end, I just settled on a pay-as-you-go plan. It's only $29.99 a month, and any unused credit I can roll over to the following month. I also have Cingular's free cell-to-cell talk time to other Cingular customers. A couple of my friends use Cingular too, so it works out really well. I don't know why more people don't get together with their friends and take advantage of this option.

I do text as well, sometimes more than I call, mainly because I find it less intrusive, and my friends can just check their text messages when it suits them. **Lily, 26**

A pay-as-you-go plan works for Lily, but locking into a capped plan can be a good idea if you are racking up big phone bills each month, as Jennifer found:

I took up the payment option to have a $99 capped bill each month. I took this out when I was living in another state, because my bills were around $200 a month. So I decided that a capped monthly amount was definitely better. What's great is that it is not a contract plan, and the only obligation is the cost of the phone, which was quite cheap. I'm not locked into any contract, and I like that. I move a lot, and I don't want to keep getting a new number each time I move, like I would with a landline. My cell number stays constant.

I pay $99 a month, which would be a bad deal if I ever used less phone time than this—but I never do. So in the end I'm making the same number of calls and saving about $1,200 a year. **Jennifer, 24**

Package your minutes

Another option is to purchase "minute" talk time, like Pam:

When I was looking for a phone plan, I found there were so many options. Some packages came with the phone, others you had to pay for a phone on top of the package. I opted for a package deal in minutes. I decided to go with T-Mobile, paying $40 a month. This got me 1,000 minutes in total, plus "anytime" minutes on the weekend. Basically, I could call anywhere in the United States, and it still only cost me $40 a month. This was in excess of what I needed, but it was one of the cheaper deals.

I found that a favorite pastime of mine is using my cell phone. Texting costs me extra. **Pam, 36**

Ring tones: why you may want to tune out

You are an individual and you want your phone to reflect this. That makes sense. The way your phone looks, feels, and sounds can be a reflection of your personality. But getting caught up in the hype of having the latest hit on your phone each week can be costly. If you think that the charges are not significant or if you're not sure how much you're spending this way, take a good look at your next phone bill.

Tips to reduce your phone bills

Choose a phone payment to suit your lifestyle. For example, a pay-as-you-go plan or a prepaid phone card offers the best value for occasional users, while heavy users are better off with a contract, like the "minute" package or capped plan to manage your cell charges. You'll also need to establish whether you're more of a text messager rather than a frequent caller, and shop around accordingly.

Don't overlook voice-mail retrieval costs. Retrieving messages can prove costly. Some plans offer free voice mail and retrieval. If yours doesn't, shop around.

Don't forget the free talk time within networks. This is great if you have friends, a boyfriend, or family with whom you are constantly in touch and can coordinate to be on the same network. Visitwww.ecellphonefamilyplan.com and compare.

If a monthly plan is best for you, then visit the Web site www.cell-phone-plans.org/providers. You'll find a comprehensive list of cell phone providers and plans.

Try wherever possible to use a landline. If you know that you'll be home or back in the office soon, then wait to make those nonurgent calls. On the other hand, if you are barely using your landline, why not consider getting rid of that phone altogether, and save on the monthly bill?

Always check your phone bill and contact your provider if you see any suspicious charges.

THE WORLD IS YOUR OYSTER

Travel is a dream that motivates many people. Your school years are over, and you are now working and earning your own money. You have the world at your feet. This was certainly how I felt in my early 20s, with a strong desire to spread my wings and find adventure.

Tina is currently planning her own adventure. She and her boyfriend are saving together, and are well on their way to achieving their goal. She has found that cutting back on those small daily expenses—a coffee here, take-out there—has really made a big difference. And she just has to think of her planned six-week vacation to Australia to stay focused.

Going overseas is the big motivator for my saving. I have budgeted to spend only $25 through the week on top of the $25 I put aside for my public transit pass. I have been doing this for the last six months or so. But don't worry, I'm not starving myself! I bring food to work each day from our weekly grocery shopping. It also helps that there aren't many places to go for lunch near my office, so I don't feel like I'm missing out. It's an effort to get into town to shop at lunchtime as well, so it's not too much of a temptation.

My boyfriend and I are saving together. Our aim is to have about $12,000 between us after 12 months' saving. We are at the halfway mark now, and so far we are on track.

If I really need anything, like clothes, I do try to find it at a discount store or wait until it goes on sale. I'd rather buy one thing I really love and wear it a lot than buy a few cheaper things that I don't like as much. I know that I will have more spending money when I'm in Australia, so it's really not that hard to avoid temptation. I wish my travel plans were as organized as my budget! **Tina, 25**

Booking travel online

Years ago, the only way to book travel was through a travel agency. The agent would take your booking details, recommend places to visit and stay, and seek out the best deals for you. Their job was to take all the hard work out for the traveler. Things didn't always go as planned, but at least you had a brick-and-mortar business to go to if something went wrong.

Now most people will do at least some of their travel booking online. Doing it this way has many advantages: you can do it in the privacy of your own home at any time that suits, and cutting out the middle step often means you save money. Trawling through hundreds of Web pages can be a little mind-numbing, though, so a recommendation is always a good place to start.

And a little caution goes a long way with online travel shopping, particularly if you are booking and paying for something that is on the other side of the world. Lots of people make bookings online and have no dramas whatsoever. But some Internet sites leave a lot to be desired, as one couple traveling to Paris found.

Aiming to book a museum pass ahead of their arrival, to save time and money, they found what they thought was a reputable site and ordered and paid for two three-day museum passes, for a total charge of 88 euros (about $110).

They received an e-mail confirmation saying the passes would be waiting at their hotel. But the passes never arrived. There was a phone number on the confirmation e-mail and, since they didn't speak French, they asked their hotel receptionist to call it and check. She tried several times, but no one ever picked up. They began to realize they had fallen for a scam.

Back home, they found that their credit card had been charged the full amount. When they tried to e-mail the address provided for queries, their e-mail bounced back. They phoned the Paris number again, but of course there was still no answer.

The lesson here is that anyone can fall victim to a scam, but you can cut down the chances of it happening to you by making sure there is a phone number on the site you intend to book through and calling it to see whether anyone answers before you start providing credit card details. The amount you spend on the call is insurance against losing much more of your hard-saved money. Another good tactic is to only buy from sites you can access through government tourism sites—they are likely to be the real deal.

Best travel Web sites

It almost goes without saying that there are plenty of great travel deals online. To help you start looking, here are a few tried and tested sites:

- hotels.com
- travelocity.com
- priceline.com
- magicalholidays.com
- expedia.com
- hotelclub.com
- fodors.com

For something a little bit different, try:

· karenbrown.com
· cadoganguides.com

If Asia is your thing, then this site is worth a visit:

· elephantguide.com

Lonely Planet's series of books cover most countries. They offer insight into the places to stay and eat, and they are particularly good if you're on a budget. See www.lonelyplanet.com for more information.

Another valuable source on overseas travel is the series of travel books called "The Practical Nomad" by Edward Hasbrouck (www.hasbrouck.org).

The U.S. Department of State issues important travel and insurance tips, including information aimed specifically at travelers. For the latest advice and warnings on trouble spots around the world, visit www.travel.state.gov.

Travel insurance

Don't even think about going overseas without travel insurance. We take a lot for granted when we're in our own country, but you can't do that elsewhere. If you're traveling in a foreign country and you lose your luggage, get sick, or have money or goods stolen, your whole vacation can be ruined. But if you have travel insurance, you can get help at the time and replace any remaining items once you're home.

And then there are medical emergencies. An emergency hospital visit is not free anywhere. Even simple problems can cost you thousands of dollars if you're not insured.

Andie is a travel agent who had always recommended travel insurance to her clients, and one day found out just how useful it was:

A few years ago I was at the San Francisco airport waiting for my baggage to come off the carousel. As the bags came out, everyone started noticing items that had obviously come from someone's damaged luggage. We were all snickering, until I noticed a familiar Mickey Mouse piggy bank and saw it was broken. I thought, "Wait a minute, that looks like the one I bought for my nephew." Slowly the other items came around and of course I realized they were my possessions, my clothes, and more gifts for my family back home. I was so embarrassed. I tried not to make it obvious, but I felt like crying.

I then saw my luggage, and it was ripped in half. I picked up the pieces and tried to pick up all my possessions as well. I went over to the baggage counter and told my story. I was half laughing and half crying.

I've always had travel insurance, but never had to use it until that day. I knew they could not reimburse me on the spot, but United Airlines was very good and gave me a statement acknowledging that my bag was damaged and that I had lost things that were not on the carousel.

I made sure to take a note of everything I lost. This was important, since I knew by the time I got back home I would have forgotten. When I got home I obtained a claim form and completed it accordingly. Luckily, I still had the receipts for the gifts and I sent them in with the form. I also kept a photocopy for myself.

A few weeks later, I got a check covering everything I'd lost. Luckily it was my sports bag that had ripped, not my main bag, so it was a relatively small amount—around $450. But that was a lot more than the cost of the insurance. **Andie, 34**

If you can't afford travel insurance, then you can't afford to travel.

Here are a couple of useful sites to start you shopping around:

- travelers.com
- travelguard.com

COLLEGE FEES AND STUDENT LOANS

A little while ago, a leading breakfast radio show ran interviews with a group of students about the impact of student loans and how they thought their student loan debt would affect their future. Most believed that by age 30 they would be earning $180,000 a year and have two cars. Some even thought they would be retired by then.

Most of those interviewed were around 18. They're certainly allowed to have big dreams, but during the show, callers rang in to let them know that the reality was very different. One 30-year-old who called in was a lawyer, earning around $55,000 a year and still owing $60,000 in student loans. Another, aged 30, owned a medical company and was married with two kids. He was earning $200,000 a year but worked a 70-hour week and sacrificed a lot for his business. Another caller was a fashion student who, after six years of school, realized her average earning potential was just $35,000 a year.

The big dollars don't necessarily follow once you have completed your degree. They may come later with experience under your belt. In the meantime, you have that student loan debt. So what are the options?

Payment discounts

It's graduation day, and all the years of study are behind you. Short of qualifying for a scholarship, most graduates who enter the workforce will have a student loan to contend with. The future is looking rosy, but the loan is hanging over your head. Thank goodness you've got a six-month grace period before you have to start paying off your loan.

Before you commence repayment, it's worthwhile to check out some of the discounts available. Visit www.smartmoney.com/college/finaid or www.finaid.org. They'll save you thousands over the term of the loan.

Here's an example of the discounts you can expect if you pay on time and you set up automatic payments:

1. Direct payments: authorize automatic monthly payments of your loan from your checking or saving account and save 0.25 percent.

2. If you make the first three or four years of
    scheduled monthly payments on time, you can
    expect to get a full 2 percent reduction on the
    interest rate for the remaining term of your loan.

Bailey decided that once she started working she would
take advantage of the discount payment plans offered to
students and put savings from the money she earns in her
part-time job into a term deposit earning 5.5 percent.

I'll finish my law degree next year and will have a student loan debt of
$45,000. Before I enrolled in college, my parents and I discussed
whether they should pay the first year up front. We decided we would
leave it until I was earning a decent salary. I didn't want to put so much
financial pressure on my parents. I'd done some investigating and found
that I could cut my student loan interest rate by more than 2 percent if
I took advantage of payment discounts. The other saving was, if I set up
an automatic monthly payment, I'd get an additional 0.25 percent off
my interest rate. I was relieved to know that I could reduce my interest
rate if I stuck to the payment plan, so I figured I could wait until I was
earning a full-time salary and not put pressure on myself or my family.

I work in a department store one or two days a week. When I started,
I set up a term deposit and have half my pay put into this account. I earn
around 5.5 percent interest, and I don't touch this money—I want to
save for a car. When I get a job in law in about two years, I will start my
student loan payments. **Bailey, 26**

Even if you have other debts, it's important to maintain payments on your student loans. For instance, Tylo has just finished a marketing degree and owes $40,000 in student loan fees. She also has a $2,000 credit card debt and savings of around $6,000. She recently started a new job. She asked me for advice on the best plan for her money.

As I told Tylo, she should pay off her credit card debt completely and maybe keep the card for emergencies—her credit card has an annual percentage rate of 18 percent, while her student loan is currently around 8 percent. As you can see, it makes sense for Tylo to pay off the credit card as soon as possible. Equally important, she must maintain her student loan payment to take advantage of the discounts.

A student loan may be one of the biggest loans you'll ever have in you life, short of buying your own home. Life can get fairly complicated when you add credit card debt to the equation. I can understand how easy it is to be swayed to sign up for one credit card after another. The down side is you may find you're in way over your head, just like Josephine. Luckily, she sought the advice of her good friend, Bree, and within 18 months, Josephine's future was beginning to shine. As I always say, power to the friends!

After completing a B.A. in journalism, Josephine found she had large credit card bills on top of her student loan to pay:

When I completed my degree, I walked out with a $40,000 student loan and debts on my credit cards, around $15,000. I did the foolish thing of juggling five credit cards at a time. I really got caught up in the hype when I took up some of the credit card offers. Once I walked into Gap and signed up for a credit card because I could get 10 percent off my purchases. When I look back I can see I was living very much on borrowed money, hoping that I would pay all my debts back once I got a job. I can remember doing the right thing and paying $100 off one of my credit cards, and soon as a sale came out I'd say to myself, well I've now got $100 to spend. It was a vicious cycle.

I'm almost 30, and I couldn't believe I had all this debt to pay and nothing to show for it. I even remember thinking I'd marry someone who would pay it off.

Two years ago, when I started with my company, I was working as an editor's assistant, earning $35,000. I have since moved into a more senior role. I'm aiming to earn $50,000 within the next two years. I've maintained the minimum payments on my student loans, but I have struggled to pay off my credit cards. I started feeling really desperate and began to wonder if I could ever buy a place of my own. One day I was talking to a friend of mine, Bree, who had always been good with money.

Right away, she made me hand over all my credit cards, and I was not allowed to have them unless it was an absolute emergency. "What about my student loan?" I said. "I really need to pay this off." She made me see that I was paying around 18 to 21 percent on each of my credit cards; my student loan rate was much cheaper. I paid off the first credit card with the least on it; now I was down to four cards. Strangely enough, this felt really good. I then paid off the next one. I also did some practical things such as riding the subway to work rather than driving, and I brought lunch from home, and used the money I saved to pay my credit card debt. After 18 months, I am now down to one credit card and I have just increased payments on my student loan and am paying off the principal, not just the interest. Also, because I have kept up my student loan payments over the past three years, I now qualify for a reduction on my interest rate. I still have some years left to pay off my student loan, but now when I look to the future I really believe I can put money aside to buy a place of my own. **Josephine, 29**

Getting your employer to pay
Elena's employer was happy to support her studies, with a few conditions attached.

I had been in the workforce for about eight years when I decided to go back to college to finish my degree. I decided to do it part-time because I have a full-time job with a large finance company. Our company has a policy that if you are taking a course that is in the same field as the work you do, then they will reimburse the fees. My finance degree fit the criteria, so there was no problem getting my employer to pay.

They agreed to reimburse my college and textbook fees on the provision that I pass each course. If I didn't pass, they would not reimburse me, and if I decided to leave the company before I finished my degree, I had to pay back the last year's fee my employer had covered.

I'm now in my third year. It is fantastic that the company has reimbursed me because it made it easier, but on the other side there is a lot of pressure to pass each course. Still, it's great they are willing to do it. College is so expensive, and when you're working and paying off a mortgage, this helps so much. **Elena, 32**

If you work for a large organization, then your human resources department will be aware of the policy on reimbursing college fees. If your company has a good intranet, it might be listed there. In some organizations, reimbursement is agreed to at the manager's discretion (if you're seen as a great asset to the company, this may be part of the incentive program they offer you in order to keep you). If you work for a smaller organization, it will probably be harder to arrange reimbursement, but check with your immediate supervisor to find out. If you think you might be interested in further study at some point and you are in the process of interviewing for a new job, ask about the policy on training and fees.

Would you consider doing this?

Savvy girl Veronica bought a three-bedroom house in order to supplement her college fees. She made this clever move with money she had saved and thanks to some help from her mother:

I bought the house when I was 20, largely due to the influence and advice of my mom. I was studying at college, and there was an opportunity to buy a property and rent the rooms out to other students. I had some savings from working part-time. With that and some money I borrowed from my family, I had enough for a deposit, so I applied for a loan. The house had three bedrooms, so I had two friends renting from me to pay the mortgage, and I was able to live rent-free.

I still have the property and I rent it out. I am so glad I did it back then, because now that I am working I do spend a lot. I love clothes and shoes. I also spend about $80 traveling to and from work; sometimes I'm running late and I'll get cabs. I also buy my lunch every day and I do have a very busy social life.

This doesn't worry me so much, because I know I have a house. I'm in a better position than my friends because I have savings (in a mutual fund) and the house. I can spend, knowing that I have all that behind me. Some of my friends spend and don't have anything. We're planning a trip to Aruba in two months, and for me the money this will cost is no problem. I really enjoy my life; I can take trips, buy nice clothes. I did get carried away with my credit card and racked up $8,000. I knew I was going too far, and now I've put the card away and have a payment plan. I've paid half, and I'll have the rest paid in three months. **Veronica, 28**

While this is a little bold, even unusual, it has proved to be a great move for Veronica. Today she enjoys the fruits of her savings and is able to spend on the things she loves. (Yes, she has gone a little overboard on her credit card and she could use the money in her managed fund to pay off her debt, but given that she is on track to have it paid off within three months, she's probably better off leaving that investment alone.) If your parents are prepared to pay for your education, then why not consider using this money for a deposit on a house in which you can have renters?

WEDDING BELLS, WEDDING BILLS

The time has come when your treasured friends no longer take center stage in your life. You don't say "I" any more. It's been replaced by "we": "We are going there"; "We are looking at a place to live"; "We did this"; "We did that"; "We are getting married."

Fabulous. But getting married is stressful. I almost fell off my chair when I read recently that the average wedding costs between $20,000 and $30,000. No wonder it's a strain for the couple and their families.

I have never met a bride whose skin hasn't broken out on the day of the wedding or at the very least who hasn't lost sleep over the cost and the arrangements. It'll happen to you, too, unless you plan to elope. But if your intention is to have a wedding with family and friends, you can minimize the stress by planning as far ahead as possible.

In terms of the basics, as soon as you mention weddings, you can just add an extra zero to the cost of everything. The cake, dress, and venue are all big money-spinners for suppliers.

Brandie and Greg were very aware of the way costs could spiral out of control, so they came up with a plan to keep that from happening:

We probably did things the opposite of most couples, because we had already bought our home and were living together for three years before we decided to get married.

We figured the amount we could save while we were young and earning good money was well spent toward our first home. Also, we didn't have family to fall back on, so having our wedding paid for by parents was not an option.

We were really happy that we reached our goal of buying our home. Then when we decided we wanted to get married, I didn't find the extra saving hard at all. Buying a house—that really teaches you how to save.

The first thing I did was put a budget together on an Excel spreadsheet. I put down a figure of $20,000, which was the upper limit we wanted to spend. I listed all the costs associated with the wedding. Each time I paid for something or got a quote, I would put this on the spreadsheet and it would calculate how much I had left. I found this helped enormously.

I limited the amount I wanted to spend on my dress to $2,000. A friend is a makeup and hair stylist, and she did the makeup for me and my bridesmaids. I spent my lunchtimes looking at ideas from Web sites, and at invitations. In the end, I did the invitations myself, which saved around $1,500. Most of the money we spent went to the reception. We had 120 guests. Quite a few had traveled across the globe to join us, so we wanted a venue with great food and atmosphere.

My advice is to be realistic about the cost. It will be very expensive, particularly if you are after a traditional wedding with lots of guests. As soon as you tell a supplier that you are getting married, they mark up everything by 100 percent, whether it's the cake, dress, or hairstyling.

Buy or borrow some bridal magazines for ideas. Be careful about additional charges from photographers—you may think that you have paid for the photos of your wedding, only to find each print is an extra cost. Speak to your friends who have been married. Use word of mouth, particularly for flowers, makeup, and hair, as you really don't want to be stressed about the way you look or feel on the day. Also, you don't want to feel as though you've been cheated. I know it's hard, but try not to make decisions based on emotions. **Brandie, 30**

Would you have your wedding sponsored?

This story may seem a little bizarre, but it worked for one couple. Having decided it was time to get married, they didn't want to ask their parents for the money and didn't have enough themselves, so they came up with an innovative idea: why not have their wedding sponsored?

They approached local businesses and asked if they would like to donate their goods or services to their wedding. In return, they would promote the sponsors to the 180 guests.

It turned out that local businesses were only too willing to help. All the couple ended up paying was $7,000 for the reception and the bride's wedding dress. The total value of everything else, which was donated, was $40,000. All the sponsors were thanked and promoted throughout the event. Okay, okay, maybe it's not for you, but you have to give them ten points for originality and for making it a success.

Over the last four years, I have seen three of my sisters get married. Naturally, there were moments of frustration and anxiety, but what got them through was their careful planning. There are some great Web sites to get you started. One I particularly like is www.ezweddingplanner.com. It's amazing—I wish I'd had something like this when I got married. It is so comprehensive; everything from protocol to vows. For starters, there is a budget page. This covers every little expense, everything you could possibly imagine, and it's easy to use. The wedding planner itself will help you keep track of all the must-do details leading up to your wedding date. You can add your own to-dos as well. You'll receive an e-mail of your planned items as they become due, so you don't forget anything. Having recently gotten married, my sister Rhonda shares her experiences:

I know you should be over the moon when your partner asks you to get married, but as I mentioned earlier [in chapter 2], I was really scared, because we didn't own anything at the time. You have this picture in your mind of couples saving together to buy their house and car. We didn't have any of this when we decided to get married.

We had to wait almost three years after Michael proposed, because we had to get our act together. We bought our two-bedroom apartment six months before we were due to marry, but even after we bought it we kept up our routine of putting $400 a week into the account we'd used to save our deposit. In those six months, we had saved several thousand dollars, and we both received tax refunds, which went straight into this account.

I figured the wedding was going to cost $22,000. Unfortunately, we were short by $10,000, although we still had a little bit of time to keep saving. As timing would have it, we received some sad news that Michael's grandmother had passed away. We also found out that some money was left to him. The money was literally sent from heaven (although we would have preferred Grandma to be at our wedding). We put this money straight into the savings account and did not touch it.

The best thing I found to help me keep on top of the wedding budget was this fabulous Web site: www.ezweddingplanner.com. I downloaded the wedding planner and put in the amount we had budgeted for. There is so much to shell out for before the wedding—deposits for this and that, the cake, and the reception. I was able to keep track of what was going out and how much I had left. I would also get reminders when payment was due and what I should be doing three months out, two months out, etc. It's really worthwhile having something like this. There is so much to think about, especially if you decide to have a big wedding.

We were fortunate that family members gave us cash as wedding presents. This almost paid for the reception, and even though we spent a lot of money on the wedding, we still had $8,000 left. We would have been able to save the amount even without the help of Grandma, but it really took the pressure off. **Rhonda, 34**

THE TO-DO LIST
Agree on a budget
The last thing you want to do with your future husband

is start your married life fighting over the cost of your wedding. Unless your parents are going to pay for the wedding and money is of no concern, you should agree on how much you are prepared to spend.

Your idea of the perfect wedding may be to have 20 close friends and family celebrating in your garden or 200 guests at a ritzy hotel. No matter what you have in mind, agree on a figure and put everything into the budget planner.

Get real figures

Visiting sites such as the one mentioned above will help you keep within your wedding budget. For instance, let's say the budget for your wedding is $20,000. You can set up a spreadsheet, put this amount as the total, and enter all the costs along the way. This will keep track of all your spending and help you stay within budget. Talking to friends who have recently gotten married will give you a realistic idea of your likely expenditures. My sisters have become experts and have saved their friends hundreds, perhaps thousands, of dollars.

Learn to compromise

Let's be honest here. If you're getting married, then, like every couple, you've already learned the art of compromise. Compromising in some areas of your big day can work wonders with your wedding budget, especially if it's tight.

You can save on some areas and splurge on others. You may not want to skimp on your wedding dress, but you could save money by making your own invitations. There are some great software packages and Web sites to help you design an invitation. For example, any home or office printer can provide a professional finish if you have quality stationery to print on. Opting for a reception with finger food and cocktails instead of a sit-down dinner means you can afford a fabulous venue instead of an average one. You get the idea.

$550

CHAPTER NINE

IT'S TRUE: MONEY MAKES MONEY

Once you have your money problems under control, you need to know about investing. If that sounds scary, relax— it's not. Even if all you want to do is open a savings account and start a savings plan, you are ready to invest. But it often sounds much more complicated than that, and boring and intimidating to boot. And if you're still in your old mind-set, it also sounds totally uncool. It's easy to get scared off.

I think a lot of finance stuff is directed at men, as opposed to young women. I'm not saying there is some big overt sexism going on here, but it does feel like you are in an arena where men know more about finance. Being able to identify with them would be good. **Roberta, 27**

Take heart, Roberta. A study looking into the number of individuals owning shares shows that half of the American population owns shares, either directly or indirectly through things such as mutual funds, and many of these are women. So women are getting more involved—investing is no longer the sole domain of men. If you feel left out, don't forget that you probably already own shares in your 401K fund.

And shares are only one investment option. You can start off small to get used to the idea:

When I was younger, my dad tried to tell me about saving, and how you should think about wealth generation. I didn't pay attention. I had this really negative attitude toward money and talking about money. I didn't like people who were concerned with money. But now that I am 25 and working, I've started to realize that this attitude hindered me, and refusing to learn about it wasn't going to work either. I decided, whether I like it or not, money is something you can't really avoid, so you might as well try to understand it. I called my dad a few months ago and told him I want to develop a savings plan. He said, "I don't care what you do with the rest of your money, just get into the habit of putting some away." So we opened a savings account. I now have 10 percent of my salary put into it each month. **Alisha, 25**

Alisha has made a great start with minimum effort. It's little steps like these that will set you on the path to really becoming savvy about investing.

Right now you are probably having a great time spending the money you work so hard for. But at some point as you get older, you may look back and say, "What have I got to show for all my hard work?" That's what happened to Lourdes.

From the moment I started working, I wanted to travel. I have traveled just about every year for the past eight years. It wasn't until I reached the age of 30 that I realized I had nothing to show for my years of working. I didn't own a car, and I've been renting since I left home. You might say that 30 was a turning point for me, because it was then that I got a little nervous about the future and what I've got to rely on. I know I have my pension plan, but from what I keep hearing, I wonder if that's going to be enough. Will I be able to keep traveling when I retire? This is something I'm really passionate about.

I've been renting for so long, I thought it was time to start saving for a place of my own. The first thing I did was open an interest-earning savings account. I want to use this money for a deposit on a condo. I have $600 taken out of my salary each month.

I hadn't been in a long-term relationship for over five years, and that was another factor in wanting something secure for myself. In about six months I'll start looking for my own place.

A few months back I met a guy, and our relationship has really grown. He is really supportive of me saving money and of my goals. I'd like to think he is the right one, but we'll just have to wait and see. Either way, I'll have something that I can call my own. **Lourdes, 32**

ARE YOU DESPERATE AND DEBTFUL
OR READY TO INVEST?

Before we move ahead, a caution: if you are struggling to pay off your debts and losing sleep over them, then you are not ready to invest. Not yet, anyway. Clear your debts first. On the other hand, if you have some money lying around, then read on. If you're stuck in the middle—in other words, you've plateaued and you're covering your expenses but don't have much left over—use some of the tips from chapter 7 to start saving so you do have money to invest.

Simply put, if you are thinking of investing and you are still paying off debts, then the answer is no. Your priority has to be paying off your debts, and then you will be able to start investing with a clear conscience.

TIME IS ON YOUR SIDE

You may not have considered this, but you are probably in your best earning years right now. If you are between 25 and 35, you are more likely to be single, in a well-paid job, and have minimal debts. Compare this to the next stage, when you may be married and have a mortgage and small children. Your budget will be stretched to cover many more expenses.

If you are single and in a well-paid job, this is the perfect time to learn about investing and understand why it makes sense to start now. It was a lesson that I learned.

I caught the investing bug at the tender age of 24. This happened purely by coincidence and, on reflection, was a huge risk for me. Before you start, you'll have to determine whether you are risk-averse or a risk-taker. I discovered I am a risk-taker. (Today I'd like to say I take calculated risks.) I am glad that I am—if I hadn't been, I would not have bought my home and built up other investments.

When I was 24, I was given a "hot share tip" by my brother. At the time, gold shares were very hot, but choosing the right one was tricky. I didn't have a clue about investing, but I was interested. I handed $5,000 to my brother, who then proceeded to invest the money in gold-mining shares. (Naivety, youth, and stupidity is all I can think of when I recall these events. Never would I do that again!) Sure enough, I struck it big with these shares, but it was beginner's luck. My $5,000 became $10,000 in a very short time.

That was my first step on the road of investing. In the early days, I thought myself a casual investor and only took a gamble on recommendations from family and friends. I sold the gold shares; the value had reached a high of $15,000, then started dropping. I sold them when they were worth $10,000 and used this to invest in my first home. My money was now making money. (It is important to note that while my first investment was a success, not all have been. Another gold-mining company that my husband and I had shares in went bankrupt, and we lost all the money we had invested in it.)

Anyway, back to those early days. Life appeared to be wonderful. I was married, I had finally bought a home, and I had a great job in the advertising industry. Having put the money into a house, my focus switched away from investing. Until the day I got laid off.

Suddenly I had no job, a very large mortgage, and, I soon discovered, a baby on the way. Was I stressed? You bet! I decided to start my own consultancy, inspired by the entertainment maestro Walt Disney, who started Disneyland because no one would give him a job. It took several months to establish myself, and it made me wish that I had some money to fall back on. I should have kept investing.

Luckily I had plenty of contacts, and the work finally started to come through—enough to pay my bills. But the experience of having been laid off left me shaken, and I vowed to put some security behind me, in case I should find myself without work again.

My interest in the share market increased rapidly, and I started to read a lot and attend seminars through the stock exchange. I asked lots of questions and read books about investing in shares and property. Initially I did have a broker, but with the advent of online trading, I decided to do it myself. A few years later, I started an investment club with some friends, which has been fantastic. The girls are a great source of support and information. As a group, we cover more ground than someone trying to do it on her own.

If times get tough again, it's reassuring to know I have built up a pool of resources.

Money makes money. That is not to say you have to be wealthy before you start investing, but investing can make you wealthy. Of course, there are risks involved. First, determine what sort of an investor you are; are you risk averse or a risk-taker? You need to know in order to be comfortable with the choices you make.

To start with, let's look at the four main areas for investing and the risks associated with them:

1. Cash or certificates of deposit (CDs)
2. Shares
3. Mutual funds
4. Property

CASH OR CERTIFICATES OF DEPOSIT (CDs): THE "UNTOUCHABLE SAVINGS"

My attitude toward saving I learned from my dad, and that is to put money aside for the future and do what you want with the rest. From every paycheck I put money aside into a CD for a trip I'm planning, and what's left is money to spend for the week. More often than not, I get to my next paycheck with only $3 left in my wallet. But this is okay. I don't feel as though I've burned all my money because I have put away that money into what I call my "untouchable savings."

I'm just starting out, and this money will eventually go into some sort of investment and generate some income. **Rebecca, 27**

Cash or CDs are very popular with young women. Probably because if you have a small nest egg to start with, they are easy to set up and you'll receive decent interest on the money you have invested. Compare this to having your money sitting in a regular bank account barely earning 0.25 percent.

One of the reasons cash or CDs are popular is that they are generally low risk and easy to obtain. Most banks offer certificates of deposit, returning around 4.5 to 5 percent for your investment. The return depends on how much you have invested—the more you have invested, the higher the rate of return. The length of time your money is invested will also determine the interest you receive. To get the maximum interest from your investment, leave it for as long as possible. You can have the interest you earn added to your original amount and reinvest the total automatically, or you can choose to have the interest paid out to you at the end of each period. The fixed-term part of the deal means that you agree to leave your money there for that period; if you take it out earlier, you won't get the full amount of interest.

Certificates of deposit are great if you are unsure what to do with your money or if you are building up a specific amount (for instance, a target figure to use as a mortgage deposit). If the money is just sitting in your regular bank account, the temptation to pull it out is always there. That's not to say accessing your money from a certificate of deposit is difficult—it's not. It generally only takes a phone call, and the money is transferred into the day-to-day account of your choice, usually in a day or two.

You don't have to have $5,000 to get good interest rates or even higher. Online banks are the best place to look for accounts that pay good interest but have very small minimum deposits or no minimums at all. EmigrantDirect is an example, with an account called the American Dream Saver that pays 5.15 percent interest with no minimum deposit or bank fees. You do, though, need an everyday transaction account (i.e., an account with a bank that has regular branches) in order to transfer the money in and out. You can open the account online, and the beauty of it is that the interest is calculated on your balance at the end of each day and then added to your account at the end of each month.

Jenny found one of these online accounts very useful:

Some time ago, a friend recommended I put some money aside in a CD. It sounded like a good idea, but I never had the time to get to the bank to fill out an application. Then I found that I could open an account online and earn the same amount of interest. I opened an account with EmigrantDirect. It was really easy.

I have $500 a month taken from my salary and put into the account. Also, when I have some spare cash, I add to it. I like the fact that I can withdraw money when I really need it. I can do this by transferring the money online into my regular bank account. It's not as tempting as having a regular bank account, because I don't have an ATM card to access the money. **Jenny, 29**

To find out more, start with:

· emigrantdirect.com
· bank.countrywide.com
· bankrate.com (if you wish to compare rates)

A tax reminder
The interest you receive on banked money is classified as income, so you will need to declare it come tax time.

SHARES: RESEARCH AND RISK CAN PAY OFF

I've mentioned the great experience I had in my investment club—and our timing certainly helped. We started in the late 1990s, which just happened to be perfect timing. The share market had been experiencing good times, with the value of shares rising and rising— what's called a bull market. Dot-coms and technology shares hadn't yet crashed, and there was a lot of interest in shares.

Internet trading started around that time as well. In the past, you had to buy and sell shares through a broker at a charge of $100 or more a trade. Today you can still use a broker if you wish, but you can also do it yourself very simply online at a fraction of the cost.

That has made it worthwhile to buy shares if you have as little as $500 saved up. Obviously, the more money you have to put into your purchase, the more you might earn by selling them at a profit. But there are no guarantees with shares. In dire and extreme situations, shares that cost $20 each to buy might be worth just a few cents when you want to sell them.

The golden rule of share trading is: only invest what you can afford to lose.

That is a harsh reality, but shares are different from investments like CDs, where you are guaranteed your initial investment back as well as the money you have earned on it.

Another difference between share trading and other forms of investment, such as mutual funds, is that in such a fund someone else does the work for you. With share trading, even if you use a broker, I strongly recommend learning about the market and keeping an eye on your shares.

So share trading is for you if you can live with risky investments and you're prepared to do some work. But let's go right back to the basics to make sure you understand the world you're thinking about entering . . .

What is a share?

When you buy a share in a company, you become a shareholder who owns a part of that company. For example, I own shares in a major department store. Each time I look at its grand old flagship building in my town, I think, "I own part of that company, even if it's only one brick!"

What is a dividend?

When you own shares in a company, you may receive a dividend. A dividend is like a "reward" for investing in that company. It is usually paid quarterly or biannually and deposited into your securities account. That is called dividend reinvestment, and it means you end up with more shares without having to buy them. Some newer companies may not pay dividends until they become more firmly established.

Tax

Like any return from an investment, you will need to declare money you make from shares on your tax return. You can make money in two ways—dividends or capital gains. If your shares pay a dividend, you have to pay tax on that amount. Some dividends are taxed at only 15 percent rather than at your marginal tax rate. Depending on the company you have your shares with, some companies will pay dividends after taxes have been paid on the company profits. This means you then only have to pay the difference between the tax percentage they've already taken out and your own personal tax level. Most dividends are still taxed at regular income tax rates.

Capital gains is the name for the amount you make when you sell shares at a higher price than you paid for them. If you buy $500 worth and you sell them a year or two later for $750, your capital gain is $250. There are two levels of capital gains: short-term and long-term. Short-term gains are those made within 12 months and are taxed as ordinary income. Long-term gains are taxed at 15 percent. Long-term losses can be carried forward and offset against any gains you make in subsequent years.

Take time to educate yourself, because while you are learning you have nothing to lose.

How do I decide what shares to buy?

You should be dabbling in the share market only if you understand it. I followed this rule myself, and I'm glad I did. Before I bought anything, I built up my knowledge and confidence. I spent a lot of time reading relevant books and newspaper articles and attending seminars, and I found I was genuinely interested in the share market and investing. If you're not—if it all sounds too hard—then another form of investment is probably best for you (although there is the "blue-chip" halfway step— see page 155).

Before you begin investing in shares, whether you go through a broker, do it yourself, or start an investment club, get into the habit of reading the business section of the newspaper regularly. In most business sections, you'll find share listings. These list share prices for the previous business day. It gives you the last share price traded, plus a figure for the highest price paid and the lowest price paid for each share.

Follow a couple of specific shares for about a month—perhaps well-known companies such as the major banks, or even the company you work for, if it's listed. This will help you understand how share prices fluctuate.

If you want to pursue it further, the New York Stock Exchange is, undoubtedly, the best place to start: go to www.nyse.com, then click on the "About the NYSE" link and look under education for more information. Also, under the "Industry resources" icon, you'll find a multitude of investor educational sites to visit. You can also visit the Securities and Exchange Commission (www.sec.gov) and the Investment Company Institute (www.ici.org).

One site that's worth its weight in gold is CNN Money. Visit www.money.cnn.com/services/glossary/a.html for a complete listing of every term ever used for investing purposes. This is a complete A–Z glossary.

Education with a bonus

Several years ago, I attended one of those stock exchange courses. I walked in and found a room full of men!

The first thing that came to my mind, given that I was already married, was: where are my sisters and single friends? For a minute I almost forgot why I was there.

Forget Internet dating. Say good-bye to expensive bars. Investment education sessions like this (not the weary "instant millionaire" type) are full of interesting men who are open to new things and committed to building financial security, just like you. These sessions are well worth attending for their own sake, but who knows, you may get more than you bargained for!

The blue-chip option—a halfway step

For those who like the idea of shares but not the research needed to really get on top of the share market, a halfway step is to buy what are called blue-chip shares. These are shares in companies that have a good reputation for making profits—whether the market is high or low—generally offer reliable growth over the long term, and pay really good dividends. They tend to be less risky than other, more volatile, shares. Think of them as "the set and forget." Examples of blue-chip companies are the major banks like Citigroup or large companies like Proctor & Gamble, General Electric, and ConocoPhillips.

You already know more than you think

When it does come time to buy shares, a little bit of common sense will help you predict future trends. For example, let's take a look at the housing boom we recently experienced. Ask yourself which companies are likely to profit from a housing boom. With more people borrowing more money, the banks will logically benefit, and this will be reflected in their share prices. This is just what happened recently. Another example is that during periods of strong economic growth and low unemployment, people are likely to spend more. Who will benefit? The retail stores.

It's not always this simple, but a bit of common sense still goes a long way.

Not-so-hot tips

Once you have "come out" and let your friends and coworkers know you're investing in shares, you'll find many people are only too happy to talk about their investments. And while their intentions may be well meaning, they will often want to pass on a "hot tip" that may not be so hot at the end of the trading day. My one word of advice is: caution. Sometimes hot tips are good, but for the most part they aren't.

I learned this the hard way. A colleague of mine who had been investing in the stock market for many years gave me a hot tip. He said the product was about to take off, and word would get out any day now. He has a large portfolio and regularly has discussions with his stockbroker, so against my better judgment, I went ahead and bought some shares in his so-called hot-tip company. I paid $1,500 for my shares. Today, those same shares are valued at a total of $36, a grim reminder that sits in my share portfolio in case I am ever in danger of forgetting that lesson.

ALWAYS REMEMBER THE GOLDEN RULE:
Never invest any money that you are not prepared to lose.

TIME TO TRADE

You have two options when it comes to buying and selling shares: doing it yourself online or using a broker.

Online

This happens to be my preferred way of trading shares. There are lots of online share-trading companies, including www.tdameritrade.com, www.etrade.com, and www.schwab.com. You can expect to pay around $9.95 to $19.95 for each trade—in other words, each time you buy or sell shares.

Using a broker

A broker will cost more than doing it yourself online. Even though I'm not a big fan of brokers, plenty of my friends use them and have been extremely successful. Choose one with whom you get along and who you trust. Use that great female instinct. You will be handing over thousands of dollars, so do your homework and start by asking friends or colleagues if they can recommend someone.

When you start talking to a broker, make sure he or she understands your money personality type. Are you a risk taker, or do you want to be there for the long run and invest in shares that pay you a dividend? Once you have established a relationship with a broker you trust, you can then try to expand into the different sectors of the market, which is what Lillian did:

I had saved a few thousand dollars, and I wanted it to earn better than the cash rate I'd get in a bank account. I'm not an expert in the stock market—I wouldn't know which share is doing better than another. I decided to contact a broker through a free seminar that was advertised in the paper. The company had been around for some time, so they were well established. I just didn't want to go to a broker I'd never heard of. The seminar was a chance to hear what they had to say.

I did have some money in a mutual fund and I owned property, but I wanted to diversify my portfolio and buy some shares. I went along to the seminar and found the brokers to be very professional. The information was well delivered and easy to understand. They showed us some statistics that demonstrated they had been quite good in picking trends in the market. Having done some research, I could see that the stocks they were recommending did seem to be doing well. This gave me some confidence in their abilities and to be honest I don't have the time or the inclination to research every stock. So I decided to book an appointment and meet with one of the brokers.

I met Brad, and we talked about my goals. I told him I didn't want high-risk shares. Based on what we discussed, we made an agreement that he wouldn't contact me until he had a share that he felt I would be comfortable investing in.

I told him my goals were to invest in shares that were safe enough so that in two years or so, I could use this money to put a deposit down to buy a property. After our meeting I had to fill out a whole lot of paperwork, and I remember thinking that the brokerage fee wasn't that much more than investing online. For my money, it was worth it.

I felt comfortable with Brad. I didn't feel as though he was going to cheat me or invest my money in something that I was uncomfortable with. The main thing I would say to anyone using a broker is to find someone with whom you're comfortable, someone who listens and who is not just using you to dump some shares. Don't be shy—speak up. If the first meeting doesn't feel right, just walk away. At the end of the day, you are paying them. Don't be intimidated by the Armani suits and plush offices. **Lillian, 34**

Lillian makes an interesting point about diversifying her portfolio. By this she means that she wanted to have exposure to various investment options. With any investment, you will experience high and low periods.

When you diversify your investments, you have a better chance of backing a winner than if you had all your eggs in one basket.

If you own property and have a mutual fund, then you have already diversified your investments. When property starts to boom, you'll benefit by having a stake in the housing market. If property isn't doing so well, you have your stocks. It makes sense to spread your money around to capitalize on the different areas of the market that do well at different times.

MUTUAL FUNDS: TAKING OUT THE GUESSWORK

Mutual funds are another type of investment, one that lets you invest in a range of things like shares and property without having to know anything much about them, and without having a lot of money. The best thing about mutual funds is they take out all the guesswork. When you buy into a mutual fund, you are buying in with a whole lot of other people and there's a professional manager to run it.

Each day, the *Wall Street Journal* compiles a list of mutual funds and their performances. You can track how each fund performs via the percentage it returns across a period of one, three, and five years. Also, you can visit the Web site of Morningstar (www.morningstar.com) for a list of other mutual funds.

As with any service provider, mutual funds will charge you a fee for joining and one for exiting. To find out the charges you can expect, visit www.personalfunds.com to investigate what the associated costs with the fund of your choice will be.

Some institutions offer no fees if you join online. For example, if you have an account with Scottrade Investments, you can download a prospectus of the fund of your choice and join. You can choose from a list of more than 850 no-transaction-fee mutual funds. These can be bought, sold, or exchanged online at no charge. They cover a range of different investment types, such as property, smaller companies, and international funds. You can diversify your risk by choosing to put money into a number of different mutual funds. Having exposure across a number of funds will give you the opportunity to take advantage when each sector is booming.

Another good site to help with your research is www.paladinregistry.com. It's an independent registry that provides objective information and services associated with financial investing.

Ramona chose the online option when she wanted to buy into an investment fund:

Since I had a little spare cash sitting around after the sale of an investment property, I decided it was time to aim for a little more return than the 5 percent the bank was paying on a CD. The question was, which managed investment fund was going to earn good money yet offer some security?

Being a regular newspaper reader, I began with the money section of my daily paper. I could see the U.S. economy was doing well. This was proven by many of my colleagues who, like me, were contractors and were picking up lots of new work. So I started looking for mutual funds that invested in U.S. shares.

It was a bit of a no-brainer, really. I just looked at the "Top mutual funds" section, considered the best performers, and discounted any fund manager that I hadn't heard of, then chose a couple of funds with good growth over a five-year period. No, I didn't choose the absolute top performer. To help the process, each fund has a star rating, which is given by Morningstar, an independent body with far more time than I have to assess fund managers. I did no other research, made no phone calls to a financial adviser, and did no Web searches.

I made the investment through the Scottrade Web site, which meant I paid almost no entry fees. As a result of selecting a U.S. share fund and a smaller companies fund with ABN AMRO/TAMRO, the money has grown at well over 15 percent a year. Sure, this was a great result in a time of terrific growth of these sectors, but given I felt I had chosen the best five-year performer, not the best one-year returns; I believed my chances of getting better longer-term returns were greatly improved. **Ramona, 36**

Ramona makes it sound easy, but remember that before she bought into any fund, she was familiar with investing and was aware of the booming economy. She is a regular reader of the finance pages, which helped her decision making.

PROPERTY: AN INVESTMENT YOU CAN TOUCH

Thousands of Americans became very wealthy overnight through the property boom in the last five years. Quaint homesteads and tiny apartments were suddenly worth a fortune if they were in the "right" location. Everyone seemed to be caught up in it. Conversation at social gatherings was consumed by who was selling and who was buying. If you did not own property, you would have felt very left out indeed.

Then the market slowed down considerably, bringing out all the doomsayers. But now that the dust has settled, the property market is again looking like an attractive investment option.

The appeal of property is that it is tangible. With shares or mutual funds, your money is put into a large pool with that of other investors. But when you invest in property, you can see and touch what you have bought.

And once you've done your homework and bought property, you'll have a great sense of achievement, just like savvy sisters Nell and Sharon. Sharon explains:

My friends kept telling me about the benefits of buying an investment property.

I began to think about it more seriously. I did own my car, but at the time that was all. Can you believe I was still living at home? So I didn't have a lot of expenses, and I knew that this was the best chance I would ever have to buy property. I was a little apprehensive about getting into debt, but I wanted to do it. I went to the accountant, and she explained things even further. I approached my younger sister, who was 27 at the time, to see if she was interested.

My sister Nell didn't own anything. I thought it would be good for us to do this together and share the load. If we got the right tenant, the costs would cover our loan repayment. Nell was really nervous and took a lot of convincing. I spoke to a friend who had done it recently, and she was great. If someone you know has done it and you can ask for advice, it really helps.

We ended up buying a new two-bedroom apartment close to the city. We looked at all the things like public transportation and the surroundings. There is a lovely park across the road and a marina not far away.

The place is rented out, and we have had the same tenants in there for the whole four years we've had it. I'm really glad we did it, and my accountant is particularly happy. **Sharon, 34**

This is what Nell had to say about investing in property:

Initially I was nervous of committing to an investment. I kept thinking about how I was going to keep up the payments—I didn't want to feel like I had to budget all the time and not go out.

I have a busy social life, and I do earn enough to buy what I want. I love clothes, and because I work for a large company I feel like I need to dress up for work. But Sharon convinced me to go with her and look at some properties. I knew she would do it on her own if I didn't go in with her. Once we got started, I really got excited about owning property.

We looked at a few two-bedroom apartments and settled on one about two miles away from the city. We really loved the apartment, and we even considered moving in. But the idea was to get it for investment purposes.

I'm so glad my sister talked me into buying it. I'm really proud that I did it, and I know that I have something to fall back on. It barely made a dent in my lifestyle, because we rent it out and the rent pays our mortgage. The apartment has gone up in value; it was the best thing that I have ever done financially. **Nell, 31**

Before you set off to buy property, be clear about your objectives. For instance, if you are buying a small condo that you wish to rent for the investment expense as Sharon and Nell did, you must think like an investor and not be emotionally attached to the property.

Tax

All the expenses on the property (including maintenance and the interest you pay on your mortgage) can be deducted from the rental income you receive. Many people become interested in buying investment property because they end up paying little or no mortgage costs after deductions and get all the increased value of the property as profit when they sell.

If you sell an investment property for a profit, you will have to pay capital gains tax. The laws on this have changed over time, so it depends on when you bought your property.

FEES AND TAXES

The purchase price of your property is only part of the story. On top of this, you will have to fork out for many extras (these figures are only an estimate, but they'll give you an idea of what to expect).

Title fees

When purchasing property, expect to pay around $500 in title charges. The title company or escrow undertakes the legal steps to ensure that the title on the property is free and clear of anyone having claims to it. On top of this, there are county/state recording fees, usually less than $200. These charges will vary from state to state: check with your tax accountant or realtor to confirm any anticipated charges on the property of your choice.

You can find out more about land title searches from the American Land Title Association at www.alta.org.

Bank loan application fees

Fees will vary from lender to lender, but a loan application fee can cost over $500 if the loan is approved.

State property tax

You will need to check the state property tax in your state, as this varies. Your loan provider or accountant will give you an idea of what to expect.

Agent's fees

This is usually a percentage of the purchase price, around 5.5 to 6 percent.

How much do I need for a deposit?

Most lenders prefer customers to have at least 20 percent of the purchase price of the property to put down as a deposit before they approve the loan. But if you have a good relationship with your lender, they may approve your loan with a 10 percent deposit, provided you can prove that you have the money available and you have been genuinely saving for more than six months. The seller of the property will also have to believe in good faith that the remainder will be paid on completion of the sale. This happened a few years back when I sold an investment apartment.

My husband and I had bought a small condo about five years beforehand, and it was tiny but in a great part of town, close to public transportation, restaurants, cafés, and the waterfront. In the five years we owned the place, it had only lost two weeks of rental. Even so, we decided to sell because we were incurring huge maintenance fees. And even though the building had been renovated, we knew there were some maintenance issues. After a few months, the realtor said she had a buyer. He had put down 10 percent of the purchase price and was ready to sign the papers.

At first it seemed unusual to have only 10 percent, but we thought if he had put the money down so readily, then we were willing to sell. What also swayed us was that a month earlier we had another buyer who chickened out at the last minute. Not wanting to go through that again, we were happy to take the 10 percent. The rest of the sale went through without a problem.

Why extra payments on your mortgage make sense

Any financial planner will tell you that making payments every two weeks rather than monthly will cut years off your mortgage. Why? Because you are effectively making 26 payments instead of 12. And if you make a weekly contribution instead of 48 (which is the monthly equivalent, i.e., 12 x 4), you'll chip away at your mortgage even faster.

Savvy savings tip

Some mortgage plans offer a home equity line of credit, which can help you pay off your mortgage sooner and have money available if you need it. Lillian has found this very useful:

I have an investment property, and it makes sense for me to put any extra money I have left over into my home loan account. It's reassuring to know I have money sitting there, plus it's eating away at my interest payments. Basically, the more I can keep in there, the more I can reduce my interest payments over the time of my mortgage. I'm way ahead of my payments now, and if I need the money for something like a vacation, I can take that money back out of the loan account. **Lillian, 35**

DO YOUR HOMEWORK

Before you jump in and buy an investment property, there are a few simple rules.

Know your market

If you have done some basic research, you will know what price you can expect to pay in any given area. If you are venturing out for the first time, Smart Money (www.smartmoney.com/consumer) has some great tips for first-timers. And to help you further, you can look up recent sales in the area where you are interested in purchasing by visiting Web sites such as www.realtor.com, www.buybankhomes.com, and www.dataquick.com. Also, visit your local realtors' Web sites to find out the sales in your area.

Ask yourself, Could I live here?

When assessing a property you intend to rent out, it pays to consider whether you could live in the place yourself. Does it have facilities nearby, like cafés, restaurants, and public transportation? Is it close to the major shopping malls? If you could happily live in the place, then there's a strong chance that someone else will want to live there.

Check your costs and maintenance fees

If you're thinking about buying an older house or apartment, make sure you take into consideration any future maintenance and repair costs, because you don't want to overcapitalize on your purchase. This could happen if you get hit with a huge maintenance bill. When it comes to apartments, I particularly like smaller complexes, because they generally have lower maintenance costs. Large complexes will have elevators, for instance, which are expensive to maintain, and pools and big garden areas mean extra charges because they need ongoing maintenance.

Saving to buy together

Steve and Louise made an agreement that helped them save to buy their own home:

When I met my partner, Steve, he had been living with his uncle and saving really hard to get together a deposit on a condo, even taking extra weekend work just to build up this money. He then bought a small two-bedroom apartment, just outside the city. Around the same time, my parents were downsizing from the family home, and this meant I had to find somewhere else to live, so we decided to move in together.

The agreement between us was that Steve would make the mortgage payments and I would save for our next property. We lived there for two years, and in that time I kept my side of the bargain. When I was living with my parents, I was spending my money on shoes, going out, drinks, clothes . . . life was one big party. But when I saw how hard Steve had worked to save that money, I wanted to try and save as well. I found it quite difficult at first, because I couldn't go to the hairdressers or shop as often.

But I was motivated. The condo we were in was a little ugly, and I wanted something nice—you know, close to the city. Luckily, in the two years we had our condo, it really appreciated in value. So we used the gains to buy the house we live in today.

The place we bought was the worst house on a good street. We didn't realize how much work it needed. To make the house livable, we had to spend $15,000 on top of the purchase price. We made one major structural change, and that was to remove the wall between the living room and dining room. This opened up the house and allowed the light to come through. We then had new flooring put in, and we painted the whole house ourselves.

In five years, we'll be in a position to do more renovations, and in the meantime we both feel we've achieved something really good. **Louise, 29**

Property for the single girl

I have just bought my second investment property. I don't need to have a man around. You know, a lot of my friends are not waiting for a man, they're just doing it themselves. **Enriqa, 26**

Sharing the expenses of buying a property is a huge benefit. Your expenses are halved, and for many people it's an opportunity to own a place they couldn't have on their own. But what about singles? Trish explains why she decided to take the leap to buy a place on her own:

When I was 30, I decided it was time to buy my own home. My older brother and sister were married and had their own homes, and I began to wonder if I would ever get married and settle down like they had. I'm a lawyer for one of the largest firms in the country, so even at that time, I earned a good salary—around $70,000—but I had been renting for the previous five years, so I didn't have much to show for it.

It's not that I don't know where all my money goes. I only have to look in my wardrobe. I confess—I'm a shopaholic. You could say that shopping is my hobby. After a stressful week at work, I love spending my Saturday mornings shopping. I have expensive taste, which means I tend to go for designer suits and shoes (they may be expensive, but they do last longer!).

I was in a relationship that ended a year earlier and had found since the split that it was really hard meeting a guy that I liked, let alone could imagine a future with. I was starting to worry and think to myself, I should have something to fall back on.

I started saving really hard, and in six months I had enough for a deposit on an investment condo. With the help of my brother, I began to look for places that I could buy. The only concern I had was that I was renting a gorgeous apartment in the middle of the city and I didn't want to jeopardize that and downsize to something smaller to be able to meet the mortgage payments. I needn't have worried.

I was prepared to spend between $200,000 and $250,000 on a condo. The bank agreed to lend me what I needed. The fact that I always paid off my credit card and had a good FICO score helped, plus I had a good job.

Eventually I settled on a renovated two-bedroom apartment close to the city. I liked it a lot, and the complex had eight apartments, which meant low maintenance costs. I've had the condo now for four years and never had problems keeping it occupied. The rent virtually covers my mortgage. I feel very lucky to have bought it; thankfully the condo has appreciated in value. The whole thing has been a pain-free experience.

The other thing is that I don't feel guilty paying rent now, because at least I own a property. The rent covers my expenses and the mortgage payments.

Today, the apartment still looks great and one day, when I'm tired of city living, I'll move in there. **Trish, 34**

GETTING THE RIGHT FINANCIAL ADVICE
BEFORE YOU INVEST

Okay, so now you know about some of the basic investment categories, and we've heard from women just like you who have taken the step into investing. If you're ready to do the same, where do you turn next? A financial adviser may be a good start. And don't worry if you think only wealthy people have financial advisers. A good financial adviser will want to be there from the beginning and help you to build your wealth, regardless of whether you have $10,000 or $100,000.

Finding the right financial adviser is a lot like finding a good evening dress. You may have to try a few before you find one you're happy with. But rest assured, good financial advisers are definitely out there. Seeking recommendations is definitely the best place to start. Ask family and friends, your accountant, the people you work with, and even the business manager in your office to recommend someone.

If that doesn't turn up someone who sounds like they might be right for you, try the Certified Financial Planner Board of Standards, Inc. (www.cfp.net). This site is designed to help you find a certified financial planner, and it includes some tips for choosing the best financial adviser for you. The service is free to consumers and offers a listing of thousands of licensed financial advisers around the country. If you know the name of a planner you would like to contact, you can check his or her details via zip code or specialty. Also, if you want to make sure he or she is a certified financial planner, you can check to see if he or she is registered with the Certified Financial Planner Board of Standards.

Another excellent resource from this Web site is a free financial planning resource kit. Simply download the kit or contact them at (888) 237-6275 and have the brochures mailed to you. The brochures, called "What You Should Know About Financial Planning" and "10 Questions to Ask When Choosing a Financial Planner" are easy to read with plenty of practical tips on how to choose the right adviser. They'll tell you how to figure out your objectives, what you'll need for your first meeting, what you should tell an adviser, and all you need to know about fees and commissions. They're worth their weight in gold, particularly for first-timers.

The first meeting you have with a financial planner should be free. In this meeting, determine if the person understands your financial goals—where you are today and where you want to be. Once you find a financial adviser with whom you feel comfortable, then he or she will charge a fee for the service provided. This can be a percentage of your overall portfolio (the money you want invested), or it can be on a commission basis. The main thing is for you to be clear about the fees and make sure there are no hidden charges.

Remember, this is your hard-earned money and you have a right to ask as many questions as needed to make sure the person you have chosen to be your financial adviser is working for you and not for him or herself.

Another site that cannot be overlooked is the American Institute of Certified Public Accountant's Personal Financial Planning Center at http://pfp.aicpa.org. Click on the "Resources" icon to find a complete guide to all matters of personal finance. Others worth a look include www.feeonly.org and www.fpanet.org (this is the Financial Planning Association site).

COMPLAINTS AND WHERE TO GO

If something goes wrong and you find yourself in need of assistance, there are organizations you can turn to. While they may not be able to solve your problems directly, they will point you in the right direction. Try the North

American Securities Administrators Association, www.nasaa.org, (202) 737-0900, or the Federal Deposit Insurance Corporation, www.fdic.gov. The right investment for you will vary with your tolerance for risk and the stage of life you're at. Whenever possible, you should have a piece of the action in several forms of investment. That way, you protect yourself against losses as much as possible and increase your chance of profit. But no matter which form of investment you choose, the key to success is confidence and knowledge. And the good news is you can build both.

CHAPTER TEN

KEEPING UP WITH THE HILTONS

You've got your credit card debt under control. You are making lots of small, painless savings, and you have extra money, which you are now investing. Okay, you are free to shop! Of course, we are talking about savvy shopping.

You can look like a million dollars without being an heiress. You can even have similar shopping fun to that of the Hilton sisters without the crippling bills. Follow these simple rules, and you'll discover that it's not hard at all.

TEN SIMPLE BUT SAVVY SHOPPING RULES

1. Set yourself an annual clothes allowance

In the first chapter, we looked at ways you can cut back on some spending so you can use this money for whatever turns you on. If your goal was to find more money for clothes or shoes, that's great, but set yourself a limit. A savvy girl knows she has planned for her annual allowance and can spend this how and when she likes, with no nasty surprises when the bills come in.

2. Remove the clutter

Do you have a closet full of clothes but nothing to wear? Before you go out and buy another item of clothing, go through your closet and check to see what might be lying neglected in the back. The trouble with too many clothes is you'll forget what you have amid the clutter. It's frustrating to rediscover a useful work skirt just after you've bought another.

Feng shui followers talk about the benefits of decluttering their homes. Once you get rid of the clutter, you bring new energy into your environment. The same rule applies to clothes: once you get rid of the old, you make way for the new. So to bring some new items into your wardrobe you will need to get rid of any items you have not worn for, let's say, a year. Forget "I may need it one day." The reality is you will probably never wear it again. So give it away or throw it out—or try selling it online.

3. Are you a trigger-happy shopper?

This scenario is one many of us can relate to. You've had a hard day at the office or you've had a run-in with someone. To help release some of your frustrations, you decide to hit the stores. It's understandable—we all get pleasure from buying new things. But when you shop in an emotional state, whatever you purchase will prove costly.

The last thing you want is to spend money on clothes you are not going to wear. If you are a trigger-happy shopper, the main thing is for you to be aware of your state of mind. Instead of shopping when you feel stressed, call a friend or maybe go for a walk—in the opposite direction from the stores. Or just sit in a café and read a magazine.

Become a savvy-happy shopper rather than a trigger-happy one.

4. Take a friend, not a group

It's great to go shopping with a trusted friend. A true friend will tell it like it is. If the item is not flattering, you need someone who'll tell you straight.

But shopping with a group is not a good idea. It not only slows you down (because everyone has their own shopping agenda), you'll also be bombarded with a whole lot of conflicting opinions. You know they mean well, but in the end so many mixed messages will probably lead you to buying unwisely. Leave the group-friend experience for the nightclubs.

5. Buy quality, not quantity

Savvy girls believe in buying one or two quality pieces at the start of each season. Yes, it's tempting to pick up something new every week, but it's not money savvy, and if you're buying on impulse it's probably not fashion savvy either.

I know a woman who buys a piece of clothing, usually from the cheaper chains, wears it once, then throws it out. She does it so that she feels she always has the latest look. She believes the clothes aren't even worth washing, because "they are so cheap they would probably fall apart after one wash. And they'll be out of style in a few weeks."

It's easy to see she has more money than sense. But if you're buying a new skirt every other week and wearing each one for just a couple of months, you're not really much different from my wasteful acquaintance. Find out what really suits you, buy for quality, and save money (not to mention cutting down on waste).

6. Soldes!

When I was 21, I traveled to Paris. As I wandered through the city center, I noticed a sign on a store window: Soldes. At first I thought it was the name of the store, then store after designer store the sign reappeared. I realized that I was in the midst of an end-of-season sale. Here I was in the capital of fashion, and a sale was going on! They had genuine bargains, and I bought clothes that still look great today.

If you like designer clothes, then train yourself to wait for the sales. I swear the sale seasons begin earlier and earlier each year. To keep track of when they start, get onto the mailing lists of the fashion houses. Every well-known designer store has a database of loyal customers, and they will keep you informed of upcoming sales and often give you a chance to shop before the general public.

7. Avoid the lunchtime shopping rush

The ideal time to shop is in the early part of the day, when there aren't as many shoppers out. I know that it often feels as though the only time you have available to get out there and shop is during your lunch hour. But if you give in to that feeling, you'll be madly competing with other rushed shoppers, you'll get little help from retail staff—who are at their busiest—and you'll be feeling hassled and possibly hungry—far from an ideal decision-making state. If you make yourself wait until a better time, then you'll be more relaxed, you'll make better shopping choices, and in the end you will save money. Can such a simple change really affect your monthly bottom line? Absolutely!

8. Buy to fit your real body—not your dream body

This is tough for any woman. But it's time to come clean about your body image. We've all witnessed plus-size women squeezing into tight, ill-fitting clothes. No one likes seeing that muffin-top belly hanging over skinny jeans a size too small!

Whether you are thin, plump, tall, or small, choose clothes that complement your body. You will get so much more wear out of them than you will buying an ill-fitting piece in the hope you'll fit into it "one day." Also, if you are buying clothes just to follow fashion and the look is not flattering for you, you're only wasting your hard-earned money.

9. If in doubt, leave it out

You have just tried on a pair of new shoes. You kind of like them, but you're not quite sure. Wait twenty-four hours, or at least till the end of your shopping expedition, then come back. If you still really want them then, buy them. But if you come back and you are still unsure, either bring a friend along for a second opinion or don't buy. And yes, they might be sold in the meantime. That's a risk worth taking. There will always be another pair around the corner. Reminding yourself of this when you're tempted but unsure is a tactic that could save you lots. It's so simple, but so true: if you really need it, you'll have no qualms about your purchase. If you hesitate, trust your instinct and leave it.

10. Shopping online

Savvy girls love a bargain, and what better way to find one than to shop online? No need to fight for the attention of the salesperson here—you can shop on your own time and find real savings. (By cutting out sales staff and the expense of running a boutique, the overall cost is usually much lower.)

Sure, there is a risk in buying sight unseen, although if you know the label and you happen to own clothes from this designer in your size, then you should be okay.

INTERNET SHOPPING

Buy and trade on eBay

With 21 million hits a month, this person-to-person auction Web site (www.eBay.com) is probably the most popular trading venue on the planet. There is a saying that everything has a price. You name it, and it will probably be on this site up for sale, from the expected to the unexpected. One guy even auctioned off his virginity!

Some savvy young women have sourced designer clothes and are selling them here much cheaper than the boutiques. It's really worth a visit. You do need to be cautious about payment. But it's worth noting that if you pay via a credit card through PayPal, which is owned by the same company as eBay, you'll get PayPal Buyer Protection up to $1,000.

Cosmetics

You can save quite a bit buying these items online, and there's no problem with sizing or color choice! Here are some sites I've found useful:

- drugstore.com
- ulta.com
- strawberrynet.com
- beauty.com
- cosmetic.mall.com

The products available are remarkably reduced, some as much as 50 percent off the retail price. Watch out for regular Internet specials. For a small price, they'll ship anywhere in the United States and will deliver free if you spend more than $25.

Pharmaceuticals

You can get good savings on pharmacy, vitamins, and health needs at:

- drugstore.com
- vitacost.com

(Don't be tempted by overseas pharmaceutical sites. You don't have any consumer protection if the goods are fake, and if the item is not licensed for American use, it'll be stopped by customs and you'll have blown your money.)

OTHER PLACES TO GRAB A BARGAIN

Now that you have these simple rules under your money belt, let's see where else you can find a bargain without spending a fortune.

Haircuts

Some of the major hairdressing chains are always looking for models—particularly salons that are associated with hairdressing academies—and offer cheap haircuts, styles, and colors to customers. Once you've found somewhere near you that operates like this, you'll need to tell them what sort of thing you're after. One of their trained apprentices will cut your hair under the supervision of a senior hairstylist educator.

Magazines

Can't live without your weekly magazine fix? Save by subscribing instead of buying them at the newsstand. Check out the savings to be had by ordering the magazine direct.

Secondhand or nearly new shops for vintage clothes

One girl's trash is another's vintage treasure. It's definitely worth visiting the best of the thrift stores and secondhand designer-label stores—you never know what you might find. A friend of mine who always looks fantastic is only too proud to rattle off the details of her latest find, like a Gaultier (or Prada) jacket for $10, at the Salvation Army thrift store.

Dress for Success

This is a terrific site to check out. It's been set up to help women dress for success without the huge price tag. You can also sell any of your business clothing, coats, shoes, and handbags. All items must be under five years old. Visit www.dressforsuccess.org and click on the "Affiliates" for a location near you.

Resale stores

One way to get some money back from your purchases is to sell your clothes through resale or consignment stores. Most stores will give you cash on the spot; some may give you the option of credit in lieu of cash. You'll find thousands listed in the Yellow Pages (www.yellow.com).

ANOTHER BONUS FOR YOUR DONATION

Did you know you could receive a tax deduction if you donate clothing to charity? You must keep a specific list of your donations. You'll need to figure out how much the clothing is worth, then get a receipt for the exchange. Check out www.salvationarmyusa.org: click on "donate" at the top of the homepage, then under "more," click "donate" again, and then click "receipts."

Wal-Mart, Kmart, and Sharon Stone

For basics, try to pay a basic price. If you find a good-looking white T-shirt at Kmart or Wal-Mart, stock up and save plenty.

A few years ago, actress Sharon Stone caused a stir as she walked down the red carpet at the Oscars. The paparazzi asked who had designed her outfit, which included an elegant, body-hugging, basic black T-shirt. She stunned them with the news that she'd bought it at the Gap. Sharon, your basic instinct proved a winner.

Factory outlet tours

Factory outlets have become increasingly popular. Today they are in all major cities and many large regional centers. They have become so popular that you can take special bus tours. You'll have to pay a fee for being driven around, but if you make a day of it with a couple of your friends, it can be a lot of fun. Just try not to fall for the trap of buying every bargain you see. A bargain is only a bargain if you needed that item in the first place.

There are too many bus-tour operators to list, but log on to the Web and search for factory outlet bus tours to see what's available in your area.

For those who live on the east side of New York, you cannot go past NYMAG

www.nymag.com/urban/guides/nyonthecheap/shopping/calendar has the best bargains New York has to offer. Every month, you'll be guided through New York's best annual sales.

If you live elsewhere, it's worthwhile doing a Google search to find if your city offers a similar guide.

Also, take a look at www.activeshopper.com. This is a bargain-hunter's paradise. Anyone can look for the best price on any item imaginable: you'll find pet supplies, electronics, travel, office supplies, and, of course, shoes, clothes, and accessories. This site definitely gets the thumbs-up if you're looking for the best possible price. It even gives star ratings for the products listed!

$550

CHAPTER ELEVEN

CHAT ROOM

No matter how far you are along the road from being financially out of control to money savvy, you're not alone. The questions and concerns you have are ones other women share:

RELATIONSHIPS

Keisha, 34, is starting to feel like time is passing her by. She is eager to buy property, but her partner has other priorities. Should she go it alone?

How long have you been together?
Two years.

Is this the real thing?

Yes, we're in a committed relationship. My partner is divorced and has two children. We rent a three-bedroom house, and we share the rent, which is $1,680 a month. The house is larger than I would have liked, but we need it because every other weekend we have to have space for his children.

Do you want to buy property?

Yes. I turned 34 recently, and I have started to think about us getting property. I've tried to broach the subject with my partner, but he really shies away from it. I want to talk about our goals, but each time we try the conversation is strained. He is under the pressure of providing for his ex-wife and kids, and I think he feels guilty that he has to put most of his money there and not into our relationship. I can understand that.

Do you have any savings?

I've saved $8,000, and I pay off my credit card each month. Luckily, I'm in a good job and feel stable there—that's why I'd like to buy property now. But my partner is feeling the strain of having to provide for his kids. I don't want this to hold me back . . . but am I just being greedy?

Sometimes I get annoyed because he goes out, stays out late, and then the next morning complains about how much money he spent. So I think, "Damn you, I'll go on a revenge spend." I seem to be doing that a lot lately.

What have you bought?
I bought a dog, and I really spoil her. I bought her a new doggy house, expensive shampoo, a doggy bed, and all the knickknacks. I've stopped now, but I guess I did go overboard for a while. Maybe by spoiling her I felt rewarded in some way.

You realize you could still buy property on your own, or even better, you could buy something with a family member or friend?
I've been thinking about this a lot lately.

How will your partner react if you were to go it alone?
I think he would be really supportive, because if we do end up together forever, at least I've made a start and he can come in when he feels less money pressure. I'm going to talk to him about this. I know my parents would help out. They'd be happy to go in for half, because they are eager for me to have a place of my own.

Feedback
Keisha feels she is in a position to buy property and the timing is right for her. Her job is stable, and her parents are there to help her. Keisha is doing the right

thing in seizing the opportunity to buy a place, even though her partner is not ready. It's hard to predict the future, and what if they should separate? If that happens, at least Keisha would know she has something to fall back on. If they stay together, then she has made a start for both of them.

If you feel as though you are ready to take the plunge, like Keisha, don't let others hold you back. If this is something you want to do, find a way.

SINGLE IN THE CITY

Janette is 25 and a working career girl. Where does her money go?

Typically, what do you spend your money on each day? When I'm organized I try to buy a weekly bus pass, since it saves on buying a ticket every day. If I pay as I go, it's really expensive. Another thing I spend money on is buying lunch. I really need to get organized. When I do the shopping on the weekend and have food in the house so I can take my lunch to work, then I'm happy with myself. But too often I just get lazy and then it really adds up: a drink and lunch can be as much as $8 to $10 a day—that's $50 a week! It really annoys me because it's needless. I do spend a lot of money through the week. I'm really bad at having cash in my wallet. Sometimes I get only $20 out just so I don't have much in my wallet, then I find I'm doing this often and to make it worse, the ATM fees add up. From now on, I'm trying to make the $20 last.

Do you have savings?

Yes, I've finally started doing it, and now on my payday I have 10 percent put right into my checking account. I got organized enough to do it because I was paying so much rent. I hated handing over $650 to the landlord every month. It's a big wad of cash. I decided one day I would like to be on the receiving end.

At first when I started the checking account, I would put money in, then find myself broke and take it out again. I had a conversation with my dad, and he said, "You have to be strict about it." So I decided to have the money taken out automatically and put into an Emigrant Direct account. After three months I have saved around $2,000.

I recently increased the amount being put into that account by 10 percent because I want to go to Hawaii for two weeks. I plan to go in three months, and I'm putting away $600 a month. It's really not that much and I don't miss it because it's being taken out automatically and I'm not aware of it. I'm living on whatever I have left, and then I get to go on vacations!

Do you have credit cards?

No, I don't, but I have a multiaccess card with debit card

access. Too many of my friends have credit card debt. If I don't have the money, then I shouldn't be buying, I think. If I don't have a card, I don't use one.

What is your biggest weakness?
That's easy: spontaneous shopping. If I walk past something I like, I'll pop in and get it. I don't really go shopping very often. But if I see something on sale, I will be tempted to go in. The other day, I saw a sale on Missoni swimsuits. They had all these really nice bikinis, and I couldn't pass them up when I saw they were only $59!

Going out is also a big drain on the wallet. I go out with my friends, and we go drinking and clubbing. It starts with a couple of drinks at a bar, and then it's off to a club, and then it turns into a huge evening. I do have a tendency to have large evenings out with people. Sometimes I can spend $130 to $180 in one night. It really depends. If you make a decision about partying on when you're not sober, you end up spending way more.

I get paid every two weeks: the first weekend of a pay period is great, but by the second I'm usually restricted to DVD nights.

Are you interested in investing?
I am. I do have this idea that I would like to gradually build wealth and have an investment property. I would

like to buy property with someone I can trust. I haven't met the man of my dreams yet. At the moment, I couldn't afford it on my own. Who knows—maybe I'll do it in five years or so. I'm only 25.

Feedback

Janette is enjoying life and partying with her friends. Sure, she spends a lot when she goes out and she doesn't hold back on buying something she wants, like the swimsuit, even if she doesn't really need it. But at least she is aware of areas where she can cut back, like getting organized and making her lunch. She also has the right idea in relation to credit cards. If she doesn't have the money, then she doesn't spend it. Taking her father's advice was good, and now she knows that putting money aside is really not that hard. And that automatic savings arrangement will come in very handy when she does want to invest.

SAVING FOR A TRIP OVERSEAS

Maria, 24, and her boyfriend, Paul, 26, are working toward an overseas vacation.

On a typical working day, what do you buy with your money, Maria?

I buy a weekly subway pass for $25 and keep $25 cash in my wallet for coffee and snacks to last me the week. I know it's not much, but Paul and I are focused on saving for our vacation.

Do you know how much you spend each day?
I know what I spend on a weekly basis. I budget a set amount each week for different things. So some weekdays I spend only $3 for the day, buying coffee. I usually buy my lunch once a week, and occasionally I buy snacks. If I go out for a meal on a weeknight, my rule is that I have less to spend on entertainment on the weekend.

Do you have savings?
Yes, I have a set amount that goes into my Emigrant Direct account automatically each payday, so I don't miss it. The money is for our trip.

Do you have credit card debt, and if so, do you pay your credit card off each month? How much, roughly, would you carry on your card a month?
I have a credit union credit card with a small limit. I try to pay it off right away to avoid paying interest. The longest I've let it carry over is three months; that was a couple of hundred dollars. I use a direct debit Visa card for groceries and other predictable costs.

That's great. So you have very little debt?
Yes, I prefer it that way.

Are you renting, and if so, how much do you pay?
Paul and I rent a two-bedroom apartment. I pay $520 a month, and he pays $800 because he uses the second bedroom as an office.

What is your biggest spending weakness?
I'd say last-minute shopping for clothes and shoes. I am indecisive and put off buying outfits until the day before a special occasion. I end up spending more than I expect to, out of desperation!

I know you are saving to travel. You seem pretty good at it too. Are you interested in buying investment property or that sort of thing later on?
This is definitely on the cards, but not for a couple of years—right now travel is our first priority. If we buy in the city, then we won't be able to afford to do much except pay off the mortgage.

Feedback
Maria is a perfect example of someone who follows just a few simple rules for great results. First of all, she only has a small amount of cash in her wallet each week, cutting out temptation. She takes lunch from home most days and will occasionally treat herself to a snack plus one bought lunch a week. She even has a debit card, so when she spends using the card to buy goods, the money

is taken directly out of her bank account. This means she is spending the money that she has, rather than maxing out her credit card. If Maria's habits are anything to go by, then she will have no problems saving for a house or any other investment in the future. Have a great vacation, Maria.

SOLO SINGLE ADVENTURER

Candice, 26, is also saving for a trip—a solo jaunt to Europe.

What's your saving method?
I have $100 taken out of my paycheck each week and put automatically into a checking account. I've saved around $1,500 in the last three months.

I have traveled before, and I also saved for my last vacation this way. I do find that some weeks I'm really low on cash, but I really want to go overseas—and perhaps even live in London for a while—so I have strong motivation.

I spend a lot of my money on going out. I live near the city, and I like to go to the local bars and clubs with my friends for drinks and dinner. I don't own a car, and I rent an apartment, so I own nothing of significance.

Luckily, I don't buy magazines, I don't smoke, and I bring my lunch every day. The money I have left is for going out with my friends.

Do you think because you want to travel it's easy to cut back on other things?
Yes, it's pretty easy. I was earning a lot less—working as a waitress—when I traveled the first time, and I managed it then. I earn more now as a graphic designer. I don't spend much on clothes, because I like to buy individual things that I can pick up from markets and thrift stores. Most times they're really cheap. I do love a bargain.

I don't feel the urgency to buy things, because I'm going overseas.

What about the future, once you've finished traveling?
I'm only 26, and I really find it hard to look into the future. When I look at the price of property today, I wonder if I'll ever be able to afford it. My older sister and her boyfriend recently bought a property, and it's miles away from the city. I feel that's the sacrifice you have to make if you want to buy a house. I've just moved into the city, from a rural area, and don't want to live way out there any more . . . well, for a while anyway.

Would you consider buying a property as an investment? That way it doesn't matter where it is, as long as it's good for rental returns and you could live where you like, knowing you've got a foot in the market.
Oh, definitely—that's really a good idea. A friend of mine is my age and she has done exactly that, all by herself!

Does this mean that you and your friends have decided not to wait for a guy to come along before you buy property? Do you think you may end up on your own?
Yes, I do. I've just recently started a relationship, and in the back of my mind, I think we're the *Sex and the City* generation. We might end up being single, and I know some of my friends are happy and fine with this. I think we know that we don't need someone to help us get by in life, or buy a house. If I reach the age of thirty-five and am single, I would definitely buy a place.

Some of my friends are just doing it now, buying property and not waiting for the traditional "boy meets girl and they buy a house together" scene. But I'd still like to think that I will meet someone and we'll buy a place together.

Feedback
Candice will have no problems saving for a property, having already saved for an overseas vacation. Most people who have saved in the past—whether it was for a trip, wedding, or car—have no problems when they want to commit to saving for something even bigger. It takes the same discipline; it's just the amount of money that's different.

BUYING PROPERTY SOLO
Andrea, 28, is an engineer working for a large agency. She already owns two properties. How did she do it?

Andrea, are you paying rent where you live? Where does most of your income go?

Yes, I'm renting; I pay $860 a month. I own two investment properties, and most of my money goes toward the mortgages I have on both.

Do you feel you are sacrificing a lot to keep up the two mortgages? Do you still go out and have fun?

I don't feel I make sacrifices at all. I've been fortunate that the properties I've bought give me great returns, and they virtually pay for themselves. I'm not out of pocket by much.

What got you started? It's fairly unusual for someone so young to have achieved this.

I've always been a person who lives within her means, and I earn more than I spend. By the time I was 23, which is when I bought my first property, I had actually saved up quite a bit of money. I didn't have the money earmarked for anything else, and my parents suggested that rather than having it sit in a high-interest checking account, I should invest in property, which is more solid. That's really how I got started. Then two years later, I used some inheritance money as part of the deposit to buy the second one.

Where are your properties?

One property is in the city, and the other is just on the outskirts of the city. I've never had any issues with renting them out.

So you have always been a saver; why aren't you into other things like clothes and makeup?

I've been working since I was sixteen, and I have always earned enough for my needs. It's not that I'm deliberately a saver; it's just that I'm not that extravagant. I've always had something left over, and that's what I saved. It wasn't a deliberate plan.

Is your whole family like you?

No, my younger brother is constantly in debt. He's always borrowing money from me.

As a young woman, was it easy to get a home loan from a bank?

I found the bank was very suspicious of me. I think they saw this young, 23-year-old, single female and wondered how on earth I could have that sort of money saved up. They kept saying things like, "Did you save up all this money yourself?" and "Is this really all your own money?"

Are you in a relationship?

No, I'm single, and I think this was another issue for the bank. They probably would have preferred lending to a couple. I think they see couples as more financially secure and likely to be in it for the long term.

What sort of research did you do before you bought your properties?

First, when I'm in the process of buying, I go and look at quite a lot of apartments. I get a feel for the prices of properties in the area. I'll look at 15 to 20 properties before I buy. I know the area, so I have a good feel for what the rental market will pay.

Also, when I bought my second property, it was already being rented. So it was good to know that the property I bought already had someone in it. I didn't have to worry about whether I would find a tenant.

I also look at the rental return. Basically I'm looking for anything greater than 5 percent growth each year.

Savvy tip: If you're looking to buy an investment property, it makes a lot of savvy sense if the property is already rented; that way you've already got money coming in to cover your mortgage payments.

What would you say to someone who is just starting out with a savings plan?

I have always said that it doesn't matter whether you save $5, $50, or $500, but you have to save something every week. You can start small.

It is always worthwhile having some money on the side so you can do what you want to do when the right time comes.

Apart from buying properties, what else do you enjoy?
I travel every year. This is a very important part of my lifestyle. I try to find somewhere new each time and usually take a month off. I don't stay in expensive places; I'm happy to stay in hostels. It's more about the experience, not the accommodation you're in while you're there.

What places have you traveled to?
Australia, Europe, Mexico, all the Pacific islands. My next trip is to England, Ireland, and Scotland. I have some friends there who are doing the working vacation thing.

To travel each year and own two properties you must earn a good wage?
I do—it's around $75,000.

Feedback

As you can see, I had quite a lot of questions for Andrea. For someone so young, she has an impressive record. It's true that she earns a good salary, but she is doing the smart thing and making her money work for her while she is young and has the capacity to earn a good wage. It's also true that she inherited a bit of money, but don't forget she'd already saved for one deposit on her own before this. She makes sure she enjoys her life and doesn't feel as though she compromises on anything. Andrea is one savvy cookie!

TIME FOR A CAREER CHANGE

At 33, Samantha is uncertain whether she wants to continue working as an accountant. Some fatherly advice seems to have hit home.

How important is your job?

I've been working as an accountant for more than 10 years, and for the past year, I've been looking for a change. I now realize I don't want to be an accountant for the rest of my life. The everyday processes have become so mundane and boring. And I used to work long hours— weekends and late nights. But my boss never appreciated or commented on the long hours I put in. In fact, he started clock-watching, and if I was 10 minutes late he would call me out on it. Now work is no longer a priority.

I'm not sure what I want to do, and this is frustrating. I'd really like to have a total career change and try something creative. I'm starting to think more about the future. I used to think I didn't care about owning my home. I thought I'd meet the right guy and we'd work toward this together. Now that I'm 33, I can't rely on that. My parents are at me to buy a place and stop renting. I don't want to get to 40 and still be renting, or worse still, be renting at 60 and have these sorts of worries.

What do you spend your money on?

I love clothes, jewelry, and going out. In the past I used to go out every night, Monday to Friday. I still never cook for myself. I rent an apartment in a nice area, close to the city, and I can walk to work. Most of my salary goes toward these things. I have to say, after I went to Asia last year and saw how cheap the clothes were, I am more cautious about how much I spend on clothes.

Do you have any debt?

I have no debt whatsoever—not even a credit card. I know this is hard to believe. I grew up in a family where my father paid cash for everything and hated being in debt. He has influenced me to use cash. I do have a debit card. I realized I needed some access to cash, particularly as I travel every year. I can at least take the cash out when I'm in another country with my debit card. The money is waiting in my bank account. I just prefer to do it that way.

I must be the only young, single, city girl without a credit card. My friends can't believe it. I do put away money into a certificate of deposit. I don't touch this. I own nothing, and I guess it does concern me, but I do have my parents to fall back on. If I need anything, I go to my parents. My father taught me the importance of education. Today he says to me, "Don't rely on a man, because there are no guarantees that he will be around forever." My father believes I need to look after myself.

One day I would like to think I could meet someone and get married and have kids. I know I will never give up work, unlike my mother. I love the fact that I can travel every year. It's my money. I have been thinking I would like to buy a house. It's getting older that has me thinking that way, and as my dad says, there are no guarantees even if you have a man in your life.

Feedback

At first glance, Samantha's life looks rosy, with no debts and an annual overseas vacation. And she has a great social life to boot. But there are some problems here.

The number-one issue for Samantha is her unhappiness in her job. This may be a good time for her to speak with a career counselor, someone who can help her figure out what she wants to do.

It's true that Samantha does have money and could possibly buy an investment property, but she needs to decide what she's going to do in her working life first. If she has to go back to school in order to change her whole career path, this will mean time off work and therefore no income. Samantha will need to spend some time to find the direction she wants to take with her career before she considers any investments.

$150

CHAPTER TWELVE

FIGHTING THE CINDERELLA CONSPIRACY

This book opened with one fairy tale. Let's revisit another we all know well. It's the story of Cinderella, who slaved away every minute, dreaming of the day her Prince Charming would rescue her. Sure enough, her prince arrived and whisked her away to a world of castles and ladies-in-waiting; free from chores forever.

But it's time to let go of the fairy tale once and for all. If you are pinning your hopes on being rescued from your job, you are making yourself a victim of the Cinderella conspiracy. You need to step out of your dream and wake up to the real world. I know this sounds a little harsh, but think about Gillian, who is approaching 50 and hasn't met Mr. Right:

I have a great job in the corporate world, and I earn good money. I can't believe that I'm almost 50 and I haven't met the right man. Sure, I've been out with a lot of men and even had some long-term relationships. I know we talk about meeting princes, but let me tell you, there are a hell of a lot of frogs to kiss first. Maybe I'm kidding myself, but I still hope to meet the man of my dreams.

I do spend a lot on my appearance, and my friends say I look great for my age. I guess that's where most of my money goes—on clothes and beauty treatments. I have my hair done every week. The reality is that I'm now competing with younger and more attractive single girls.

I really believed that by now I would have been married with kids. I'm so tired of working hard, and I have left it so late to start putting money away. I only started putting some money away about three years ago, but luckily I now have enough for a deposit on an apartment. Can you believe I've been renting for almost 30 years! If I had bought a small condo a few years earlier, I would have made a big dent in my mortgage by now.

My biggest fear is that the bank will not lend me the money because I'm getting older, even though my FICO score is good and I have always paid my credit cards on time. All I can say is thank God for my job. Luckily, I have some money in a pension plan piling up for when I retire.

Gillian, 49

I'm sure you know someone like Gillian who wonders how life has passed by so quickly and who hasn't found someone to settle down with. Gillian's saving grace is her job and the security it gives her. I wish Gillian the best, and it is great she has finally made a start. But I also wish she'd had a friend to give her some good financial advice 20 years ago.

WHY MARRIAGE IS NO LONGER THE ULTIMATE PLAN

Not so long ago, young girls expected to meet their perfect match and settle down to married life and children. A job of their own, let alone a career, was rarely part of the picture. Now the focus is on education and careers. It's wonderful to be living in an age when women can be and do anything they choose.

Marriage is definitely on the cards for many young women, but often not until they are in their 30s. And as we know, the divorce statistics are very high. As well as getting married later, women are waiting longer to have babies. It really is great to have a lot of options, but it means that you need to think about the fact that if you have a baby in your late 30s, you will still be supporting that child in your late 50s—all the more reason not to let your career go by the wayside.

Tania had a great job as a senior manager for a large telecommunications company, but after the birth of her first child eight years ago, she made a decision she now regrets:

When I was in my 20s, I was self-assured, healthy, and had lots of energy. You know what they say, "The world's your oyster." When you are young, you can indulge in everything: your friends, your job, and your relationship. You have time to think and to develop what you want to do. And despite the impending birth of my first child, I thought things were not going to change too much.

Up until I had my son, I thought all working moms overdramatized their situation. I worked right up until a couple of days before he was born. I really enjoyed my job and planned to go back.

But while I was on maternity leave, I was looking casually at the job advertisements and I saw a job with more flexible working hours. I thought this would allow me to leave the office earlier in the day, which seemed very attractive. I applied for it just to see what happened, and I was offered the job. I made a hasty decision to take it, and this proved to be the biggest mistake. I am now in a job where I am just another faceless number.

I know we make choices in life, and I made a conscious decision to give myself to my family (we now have two kids). I have fulfilled the family role but not my work role, which is a shame.

We have a mortgage, and I need to keep working. We have an army of friends and family who help with the kids. I'm so lucky in that respect. My husband also changed his job to take on a role within a government agency. This means he can finish earlier and pick up the children from school on some days, the other days a friend drops the kids off at home.

Now that I'm a working mother, I have renewed respect for other working moms. I sometimes think there is too much pressure to achieve it all. There is so much information that we get distracted from what we really want out of life. I now know I would have been happier in my old job—they treated me with respect. I went from running a department to a much lesser role. Today, my job just pays the bills. **Tania, 37**

Tania's story makes it clear that even when you have a family you love, work is still important. She misses the challenges in her previous job and perhaps regrets not trying to get more flexibility in a job she was happy with. For other mothers, being at home full-time through their children's preschool years is their preferred option. It's only when you're in the position of making that decision that you'll know what's really right for you. But when it comes to making arrangements that suit you and your family, your job is definitely part of the mix. As pioneering photojournalist Margaret Bourke-White put it, "Work is something you can count on, a trusted life-long friend who never deserts you."

MORE CHOICES, MORE CHALLENGES

Your parents' generation was likely to have worked in nine-to-five jobs and stayed in the same jobs for many years; in fact, often as long as 40 years, which is unheard of today.

With full-time and long-term employment becoming a rarity, your working life will be very different from theirs. A little more than 40 percent of jobs are now casual or contract, and these situations are on the rise. Today's working environment means that your career is likely to be a jigsaw puzzle put together from the following pieces.

- Freelance work
- Contract work

- Casual and part-time work
- Project work—working for an assigned period on one specific task
- Shift work—particularly in fast-growing service industries such as hospitality
- Working from home

That's fine—it suits many of us, like these career girls:

I really enjoy meeting new people, and every day there's something unexpected and different. **Isla, 29, national account manager**

I find it incredibly satisfying to identify and analyze problems with our current business operations and then successfully implement solutions to these problems. **Tina, 35, IT business analyst**

I work on interesting projects. I'm constantly learning, and no two days are ever the same. **Ling, 33, help-desk manager**

I like all the options available to me as an accountant, there are so many different career paths, industries, and locations that I can choose from. **Josie, 29, financial analyst**

But there are concerns, too. The three issues that stand out, whether you are working in a traditional full-time job or in short-term contracting roles, are the following:

1. Long hours

2.   Less security
3.   Increased pressure in the workplace

If you're feeling consistently overworked and insecure, you are not alone.

Most people now in the early stages of their working lives will have ten different jobs and three or four different types of careers over their lifetime, and the switches may not all be voluntary. Being money savvy means that your stress is kept to a minimum when those big changes occur.

Welcome to the world of actors and models

Actors and models have long been familiar with short-term work and the inevitable downtimes between jobs. Now the rest of us are finding out what it's like.

Kelly's brief working history is an example of one based around short-term assignments:

I'm only 24, but I have moved in and out of a number of jobs. I've done secretarial and restaurant work, and I've worked in a sports shoe store. I've been lucky enough to have work when I really needed it. I have my name down with a number of employment agencies. Sometimes I get anxious between jobs, but I keep in regular touch with the agencies.

I really enjoy the freedom of working on a casual basis or temporary assignments. The downside is I don't have a track record for being in one place long enough. The banks don't want to know you if you don't have a good working history. I may have a problem applying for a car loan, which I want to do, or even a credit card. Some of my friends envy me, because they think my life is flexible. It's true; I can plan to take time away—there are benefits—and I also like the variety of people I meet. I must admit, I have developed into a good saver as well. I have to be— otherwise, I can't meet my rent payments. **Kelly, 24**

Kelly is right to have concerns about the bank giving her a loan when she needs one, because she does change jobs regularly. A good track record of savings, and keeping up regular credit card payments, will help.

ARE YOU REALLY IN THE RIGHT JOB?

Think of it this way: you will spend most of your adult life working. So it makes sense to take the time to find out what you really want to do. Have you chosen the right career?

If you are uncertain about your job, one way to help clarify your options is to speak with a career counselor or career adviser. A career counselor will look at areas in your life such as your lifestyle and your income and ask you what your long-term goals are. Some organizations are bringing career counselors on board and offering their services to their employees.

If you are working for a large organization or government agency, check to see if they have someone available—start with the human resources department. Of course, you will need to be discreet, so that you are not seen to be looking around for a new job.

If your company doesn't offer this service, then check out Career Voyager (www.careervoyager.gov). This comprehensive site offers free information on various careers. If you wish to enlist the services of a career counselor or career coach, you can expect to pay anywhere from $50 to $300.

When IT manager Reba became disillusioned with her job, she decided to get some expert help. After a few sessions, she is feeling a lot happier about her future:

I've been in the IT area for over eight years, and to be honest, I really feel like I've had enough. When I started in the industry, it was exciting as new developments in telecommunications evolved. But lately the industry has just gotten so tough, and it's hard coming in every day wondering if I'll get the ax.

I decided it was time to see a career coach. I got the name from a friend of mine who had some success from using one. When I made the appointment, Vanessa, the coach, asked me a whole lot of questions, like what my goals and aspirations were, where I wanted to be, and what I valued in my job. We also looked at what skills I have. She then devised a plan to help me meet some of the goals. My goals weren't financial, as I already owned my home and I had some other investments, like shares and funds. I had always earned good money and had some sense to put money away for a rainy day.

I'm a good manager and very well organized. What I came to realize was that I needed something that would allow me to express some creativity. Now I have my sights set on opening a small lodge in the mountains. A friend of mine who is also disillusioned with her job is eager to come in as a partner. I'm really excited about the prospects. I'm starting to feel energized again when I look to the future. I hope to achieve my dream within four years. **Reba, 35**

Where to go

If you are uncertain about your career or future directions, the National Career Development Association (www.ncda.org or (918) 663-7060) is a terrific starting point. This association is national, with members who provide advice for people seeking to enter the workforce or change their work direction. The Web site has a search facility under the tab "Need a career counselor" to find a counselor in your area. Also, extremely useful for first-timers are guidelines for consumers on choosing a career counselor.

Women's organizations and networking

Networking can be one of the most powerful assets you have in your working life. Just look around, and you'll probably find you know someone who has landed a job through the connection of a friend, colleague, or associate.

Elizabeth is a journalist whose last three assignments have come through contacts:

The work I do tends to be on a short-term or project basis. Over the past five years, I've had three contract assignments. All these jobs came through industry contacts. I make sure I keep in touch with my friends and colleagues, not just because I'm after a job but because we all look out for each other. The very nature of my job means I have to keep in touch with my associates; otherwise, I could be out of a job for ages.

The other day a friend was looking for a job, and she sent an e-mail to a whole lot of contacts, saying she was available for work. She asked if we could forward her details to anyone we knew who could use her services. Within two weeks, she landed a job. **Elizabeth, 36**

There are dozens of women's networking groups across the United States. Search on the Web for women's business networking organizations.

TIPS TO HELP YOU FIND A JOB

If you are in the process of looking for a job, here are a few tips to help you along the way:

- Search Internet recruitment sites to see what's out there, how much it pays, and what qualifications and experience you'll need. Start with: www.careerbuilder.com, www.jobing.com, www.jobster.com, www.jobwire.org, and www.headhuntersdirectory.com.
- Daily newspapers—get into the habit of reading the careers sections.
- Read specialist magazines and Web sites that are

relevant to your industry or the one you want to break into.
- Network. Don't ever forget the power of friends and colleagues.
- Recruitment firms. Make an appointment with a recruitment agency that works within your field to get a feel for what is happening in the marketplace and what sort of salary you can expect based on your experience. This service is free to you (the employer pays the agency costs).
- Update your résumé. Have a friend or colleague go through it to make sure you haven't missed or downplayed anything that could be important. And make sure you're honest—don't invent things in hope of getting a job.
- When you're applying for a particular job, or if you get an interview, research the company in question. Check out their Web site and search other sources for news about them.

WORKING FROM HOME

Maybe you have decided to take the plunge and start your own business. No more clock-watchers hovering over you or pointless meetings. You're able to choose the hours you want to work, and the portable office means you no longer have to be tied to your desk—cafés have become the second office for many people who work from home.

Setting up a home office can be quite expensive, but on the other hand, you can claim the costs of running your home office against your income, provided this is the only office you have. Home-office deductions can be a red flag for audits, so keep your expenses legitimate—the last thing you want is the IRS knocking on your door. Otherwise, business deductions for expenses and travel are a great way to save on taxes.

Check with your accountant for details about what you can and can't claim.

Savvy girl Celestine, 34, decided to start her own business from home. Clever thinking and assistance from her boyfriend have helped reduce some of her setup costs.

I have been a travel consultant for more than 10 years. When I turned 33, I decided I wanted to start my own business. I'm in a serious relationship, and my boyfriend and I have discussed having a child soon. But before that happens, I wanted to make sure I was set up to work from home.

I had maintained a good relationship with my former employer. And with the help of my boyfriend, I set up a computer system and software package that enables me to log into the network of that previous employer and use their resources. This proved to be a win-win situation for me and my ex-employer, because I didn't have to buy the network software used by travel agents, which saved me a lot of money, and they get a percentage of the fee I earn when I book any travel.

Now with the business up and running, I feel that I can still keep earning income when the time comes for us to have a child. **Celestine, 34**

Make your setup work for you

It doesn't matter which road you decide to take when it comes to your career; whether you choose to be your own boss, freelance for other companies, or be part of the corporate world, the important thing is that you are able to maintain an income. Use this valuable time, while you're working, to put money aside. Remember, your earning years should also be your saving years.

$550

CHAPTER THIRTEEN

THE LAST WORD

I hope this book, and the stories you've found in it, have inspired you to make some changes in your life. It doesn't matter how big or small. Even if all you do is choose to open the "no-touch" bank account or start to pay off your credit card debt regularly, you're on your way to being money savvy.

The important thing is to just start. Once you do, there is a domino effect and other things will start improving as well. Remember how Rhonda started out with nothing and then, when she set her mind on the goals she wanted to reach, everything else fell into place?

Sure, you'll encounter obstacles along the way. That's life. The women who've shared their stories can help you see that even when things haven't been going so well, a few changes can turn everything around. And nothing beats the satisfaction you'll feel when you reach your goals.

Once you have gained some financial independence, be proud of it and help others. Don't forget, it's okay to talk about money. In fact, you're crazy if you don't—whether you have it or not. We all learn from sharing our stories.

I also hope that you'll come away from this book knowing that what's important isn't really how much you earn but what you do with it. Being rich is not just about your monetary worth. True wealth comes from being able to enjoy your friends, family, and work—in short, your life—as well as all the goodies that being money savvy will bring your way.